Democratic Alternatives

Matias Brum

Democratic Alternatives

Social Democracy, Market Socialism and the Situationist Project

palgrave
macmillan

Matias Brum
Universidad ORT Uruguay
Montevideo, Uruguay

ISBN 978-3-032-23152-9 ISBN 978-3-032-23153-6 (eBook)
https://doi.org/10.1007/978-3-032-23153-6

This Palgrave Macmillan imprint is published by the registered company Springer Nature Switzerland AG.
The registered company address is: Gewerbestrasse 11, 6330 Cham, Switzerland

"Given the profound uncertainty about the future, it makes sense to keep alive the flame of a set of normatively attractive and coherent proposals within our radical egalitarian imagination."

— Erik Olin Wright

"Was ist ist.
Was nicht ist, ist möglich.
Nur was nicht ist, ist möglich." (What is, is.
What is not, is possible. Only what is not, is possible.)

— Einstürzende Neubauten

This book is dedicated to my mother, Ana,
to my father, Fernando
to my partner, Anahí,
and to my children, Lucio and Emilio —
with love and gratitude for the inspiration they give me every day

Preface

This book explores the possibility that institutional traditions like social democracy and market socialism can act as pathways toward certain emancipatory goals articulated by the Situationist International (SI). While the SI explicitly rejected institutional politics and promoted the radical transformation of everyday life in the face of the 'society of the spectacle' (Debord, 1967), their critique of alienated labor, commodified urban space, and forms of mass consumption resonates with contemporary debates on universal basic income, the reduction of the working day, participatory urbanism, and the cooperative management of strategic resources (Weeks, 2011; Buch-Hansen & Koch, 2018; Bauwens et al., 2019).

This book does not claim to speak on behalf of the Situationist International, nor to reconstruct its revolutionary program. Rather, it mobilizes Situationist concepts as critical tools for evaluating contemporary reformist projects, including those the SI itself would have rejected. In doing so, the analysis treats the SI as a critical diagnostic framework rather than as a political blueprint, allowing its concepts to illuminate tensions, limits, and risks within contemporary reformist strategies. The SI's rejection of institutional politics is taken seriously here as a critical constraint, not resolved away.

The book develops a conceptual framework that translates Situationist concepts—such as *dérive*, *détournement*, decommodification, autonomy, and spatial reappropriation—into analytical categories that are evaluable for concrete reforms. Through empirical case studies on the reduction of the working day in Iceland and cooperative development in Mondragón, we examine both the conditions that enable material and cultural emancipation and the risks of co-optation, bureaucratization, and reproduction of the spectacle (Berg et al., 2021; Restakis, 2010).

The findings suggest that certain social democratic and market socialist reforms can generate *conditions of possibility* for a post-spectacular society, fostering collective capacity, creativity, and political participation, as long as they are articulated with broader social movements and are designed as *non-reformist reforms* that challenge the dominant logic rather than merely improving existing conditions.

This approach contributes to the literature on applied Situationist praxis and offers a methodological framework for evaluating the transformative potential of institutional interventions in advanced capitalist contexts.

The Situationists defined themselves, from the very beginning, as radically anti-reformist. This was not simply a matter of strategic choice but a constitutive principle of their project: the conviction that no truly emancipatory transformation could be achieved through incremental adjustments, partial accommodations, or compromises with dominant political forms. Guy Debord, the central figure of the movement, embodied this hostility with particular force, opposing any kind of reformism, whether "pink" in the sense of social democracy, or "red" in the sense of statist socialism.

The Situationist wager was revolutionary in the strongest sense: to transform the totality of social and cultural life, to overturn capitalism not only in its economic structures but also in its modes of experience, its urban forms, its control of time, and the very construction of desire. In this regard, the early discussions around unitary urbanism and the contested dialogue with Henri Lefebvre are especially revealing. They illustrate both the power of conceiving urban life as a laboratory of emancipation and the internal tensions over whether such radical imagination could be reconciled with forms of planning or concrete municipal policy.

It is clear that, in their own terms, the Situationists rejected any attempt to "bend" their project toward the institutions of the state, the market, or gradualist reform. And in many respects, they were right: later experiments in social democracy or market socialism could hardly be stretched into a Situationist horizon. Yet the premise of this book is different: even if the core of Situationist thought is irreconcilable with reformism, its conceptual framework remains useful when evaluating reforms, public policies, and alternatives to unrestrained capitalism.

This is not, therefore, about proposing a "Situationist social democracy"—an oxymoron in itself—but rather about using the Situationist critique as a lens. That lens allows us to perceive the limits of reform, to identify when reforms end up reinforcing alienation or the commodification of life, and at the same time to explore how some measures, however insufficient, may open cracks, experimental spaces, and conditions for freer and more creative forms of life.

In other words, the key is to keep the tension alive: to recognize that Situationism, in its purest form, is hostile to all reformism, but also to salvage from that radicalism a critical compass with which to examine proposals such as universal basic income, shorter working hours, participatory urbanism, or the social management of strategic resources. While none of these measures exhaust the Situationist promise of revolutionary transformation, all of them can be analyzed in the light of its legacy, insofar as they help imagine alternatives to the brutal logic of capital.

This book thus positions itself within that interstice: between the intransigent heritage of the Situationists and the contemporary necessity of thinking about concrete pathways of social transformation.

On a more personal note, this book brings together different stages of my own political and intellectual life. It connects the teenage anarcho-punk who first discovered Situationist ideas as a way of naming everyday alienation; the younger adult forced to grapple with the uncomfortable realities of political choice, compromise, and voting in an imperfect world; and the later technocrat who now tries to push for social democracy and market socialism as imperfect but necessary tools for change. What ties these moments together is not a sudden conversion or a clean break, but a long journey—stretching over roughly twenty-five years—of learning, constraint, responsibility, and persistence. This book is not about abandoning the Situationist critique, but about carrying it with me into adulthood, into institutions, and into decisions that have real consequences for others, where ideals must meet trade-offs and where refusing to choose is itself a choice.

Acknowledgements I wish to express my deepest gratitude to **Guillermo Alves, Andres Alsina, Santiago Beiro, Sebastian Berazategui, Cecilia Bello, Anahí Bermúdez, Fernando Brum, Milena Brum, Alvaro Brunini, Gabriel Burdin, Sylvia Caceres, Carolina Campo Lupo, Paula Carrasco, Lorena Castellanos, Emiliano Castro Martinez, Fira Chmiel, Alberto Costoya, Vessela Daskalova, Andrés Dean, Silvana di Salvatore, Virginia Esmoris, Carlos Ezquerra, Mirta Fajardo, Mery Ferrando, Sebastian Fleitas, Nestor Gandelman, Gergely Ganics, Michel Godin, Julian Gonzalez Guyer, Mariana González, Rita Gutierrez Ros, David Lugo, Javier Lopez Rios, Ines Martinez Echagüe, Adriana Martinez Perez, Carolina Mena, Daniel Olesker, Guzman Ourens, Ivone Perazzo, Veronica Perez, Santiago Pepe, Gustavo Pereira, Inti Piccioli, Sandra Piccioli, Horacio Rueda, Ana Solari, Stefania Simion, Tajda Spital, Mikhail Timonin, Emiliano Tonarelli, Carlos Uribe, Victoria Vázquez, Andrea Vigorito, Mijail Yapor, Mariana Zerpa, Leandro Zipitria**, and all the people at AGORA, CREARE, FCEA, IAVA, IECON, ORT, Queen Mary and UdelaR, for their invaluable support, insightful feedback, and encouragement throughout my life and the development of this work. Their expertise and generosity have been instrumental in shaping the ideas presented in this book.

I would also like to thank **Sarah Roughley, Christian Winting**, and all the other people at Palgrave Macmillan for their professionalism, support, and guidance throughout the publication process.

I also wish to acknowledge three anonymous referees, as well as other colleagues, friends, family, partners and mentors whose contributions and conversations have enriched this project in ways too numerous to list here. Their inspiration and collaboration have made this endeavor possible.

Competing Interests The author has no competing interests to declare that are relevant to the content of this manuscript.

Contents

1 Introduction 1
1.1 What a Situationist Perspective Adds 3
1.2 Book Roadmap 6

2 Theoretical Framework 7
2.1 The Situationist International: Critique and Praxis 7
2.1.1 The Society of the Spectacle: Theoretical Foundations and Implications 8
2.1.2 The Revolution of Everyday Life: Subjectivity and Liberation 9
2.1.3 Situationist Practices: Theory in Action 11
2.1.4 Political Positions and Strategic Orientations 13
2.1.5 May 1968: Theory in Practice 14
2.1.6 Dissolution and Legacy 15
2.2 Social Democracy: Reform Within Capitalism 16
2.2.1 The Golden Age Model: Institutional Architecture and Social Outcomes 17
2.2.2 Critiques and Contradictions: Theoretical and Practical Challenges 20
2.2.3 Internal Contradictions and Sociological Transformations 23
2.2.4 Contemporary Relevance and Renewal 24

2.2.5 *Theoretical Debates and Future Directions* 25

2.3 *Market Socialism: Beyond Capitalist Property* 26

2.3.1 *Historical Development: From Calculation Debates to Democratic Models* 27

2.3.2 *Contemporary Theoretical Models: Diversity in Democratic Property* 29

2.3.3 *Institutional Design and Governance Mechanisms* 31

2.3.4 *Practical Examples and Contemporary Applications* 33

2.3.5 *Challenges and Critiques: Theoretical and Practical Limitations* 35

2.3.6 *Contemporary Relevance and Future Prospects* 37

2.4 *Points of Convergence with Situationist Critique* 38

2.4.1 *Universal Basic Income and Decommodification: Beyond Wage Slavery* 39

2.4.2 *Reduction of Working Time and Temporal Liberation: Reclaiming Life from Accumulation* 43

2.4.3 *Participatory Urbanism and Spatial Liberation: Cities as Sites of Collective Creation* 47

2.4.4 *Democratic Resource Management and Economic Democracy: Socializing Strategic Assets* 51

2.4.5 *Synthesis and Critical Evaluation: Possibilities and Limitations of Convergence* 56

2.4.6 *Contemporary Movements and Future Possibilities* 59

3 Analytical Framework: Evaluating Reforms through Situationist Categories 63

3.1 *Framework Components and Methodological Considerations* 64

3.1.1 *Spectacle and Alienation: Analyzing Mediation and Authentic Experience* 65

3.1.2 *Decommodification and Autonomy: Beyond Market Dependence* 67

3.1.3 *Everyday Life, Desire, and Play: Transforming Daily Experience* 69

3.1.4 *Spatial Reappropriation and Urban Commons: Cities as Sites of Liberation* 71

3.1.5 *Détournement of Institutions: Subverting Dominant Logic from Within* 74

3.2 *Operationalization Matrix for Situationist-Informed Policy Evaluation* 76

3.2.1 Analytical Notes 76
3.2.2 Strategic Implications 78
3.3 Application Methodology and Research Strategies 79
3.4 Methodological Considerations 80

4 Case Studies 83
4.1 Iceland's Working Time Reduction Experiment (2015–2019) 83
4.1.1 Background and Design 83
4.1.2 Key Findings 84
4.1.3 Situationist Analysis 86
4.1.4 Limitations and Context 88
4.2 The Mondragón Cooperative Experience 89
4.2.1 Historical Development 89
4.2.2 Institutional Innovations 90
4.2.3 Challenges and Contradictions 92
4.2.4 Situationist Analysis 93
4.2.5 Lessons and Implications 96
4.3 Comparative Analysis 97
4.3.1 Divergent Trajectories Toward Social Transformation 97
4.3.2 Institutional Ecology and Support Networks 98
4.3.3 Risks of Cooptation and Structural Limitations 99
4.3.4 Criteria for Situationist-Aligned Reforms 101
4.3.5 Prefigurative Politics and Movement Building 102
4.3.6 Movement Catalyzing Potential 103

5 Criticisms, Limitations, and Responses 105
5.1 Cooptation and the Reproduction of the Spectacle 105
5.1.1 The Orthodox Situationist Critique 105
5.1.2 Response: Contingency, Struggle, and Strategic Framing 107
5.1.3 Strategic Considerations for Preventing Cooptation 108
5.2 Generalizability and Contextual Specificity 109
5.2.1 The Challenge of Context-Dependence 109
5.2.2 Response: Scope Conditions and Principles of Adaptation 110
5.3 Theoretical Translation and Methodological Fidelity 112
5.3.1 The Challenge of Conceptual Coherence 112

5.3.2 *Response: Methodological Innovation with Theoretical Fidelity* 113
5.4 *Temporal Dynamics and Structural Constraints* 115
5.4.1 *The Challenge of Long-Term Sustainability* 115
5.4.2 *Response: Building Durable Transformation Capacity* 116
5.5 *Strategic Synthesis and Way Forward* 117
5.6 *Conclusion* 118

6 Conclusion 119

Bibliography 127

Index 143

CHAPTER 1

Introduction

The tension between institutional reform and radical transformation has been a central theme in political theory, critical sociology, and cultural studies. Can institutional reform traditions, such as social democracy and market socialism, constitute effective pathways toward the radical horizons articulated by the Situationist International (SI)? This question places the research at the intersection of classic debates on reform versus revolution, institutional mediation versus direct action, and the potential for transformative change within existing political structures. Historically, the discussion has oscillated between those who argue that only extra-institutional action can dismantle dominant power logics and those who defend that strategic, carefully designed reforms can open up spaces for emancipatory experimentation without being co-opted (Wright, 2019; Holloway, 2002).

Rather than offering a comprehensive alternative economic model, this book uses Situationist theory as a critical lens to evaluate the transformative potential of existing and proposed reforms. The Situationist International, founded in 1957, emerged as a critical synthesis between artistic avant-garde movements and the post-war radical Marxist tradition in Europe. Their central critique was directed at advanced capitalism, particularly the domination of everyday life by what Guy Debord termed the *society of the spectacle* (Debord, 1967). For Debord, the spectacle isn't merely entertainment but a form of power that transforms social experience into a commodity, limiting the autonomy, creativity, and political

M. Brum, *Democratic Alternatives*,
https://doi.org/10.1007/978-3-032-23153-6_1

action of individuals. In the face of this logic, the SI promoted practices like the *dérive* and *détournement*, articulating art, politics, and everyday life, with the goal of liberating the imagination, reconstructing social bonds, and fostering direct action (Knabb, 2006; Vaneigem, 2012). These Situationist proposals radically challenge conventional institutional politics, which often reproduces underlying power structures and hinders the profound transformation of social life.

However, contemporary experience shows that certain social and economic reforms can generate conditions that evoke elements of Situationist praxis. Policies inspired by social democracy and market socialism—such as universal basic income (UBI), the reduction of the working day, participatory urban planning, the promotion of cooperatives, and progressive redistribution mechanisms—not only improve immediate material well-being but can also strengthen collective capacities, stimulate autonomy, and open up spaces for social innovation (Weeks, 2011; Buch-Hansen and Koch, 2018; Gorz, 1989). These initiatives can be conceived of as *non-reformist reforms*, in the sense of Gorz (Gorz, 1968), as they don't solely seek to adjust the functioning of the existing system but to enable practices that question its dominant logic and enable new forms of social action and collective creativity.

The link between institutional reforms and Situationist praxis is also evident in contemporary debates on post-work, the commons, ecological transition, and the democratization of urban spaces. These discussions, while materialized through institutional instruments, share Situationist concerns: promoting collective autonomy, generating critical consciousness, and experimenting with alternative forms of social organization (Srnicek and Williams, 2015; Bauwens et al., 2019). Empirical research on the reduction of the working day, cooperatives, and participatory planning suggests that such interventions not only have positive effects on quality of life and equity but can also function as social laboratories that foster creativity, collective deliberation, and new community practices (Berg et al., 2021; Restakis, 2010).

This book aims to examine the extent to which institutional reforms can create *conditions of possibility* for a Situationist praxis, evaluating both their transformative potential and the risks of co-optation or neutralization. To do this, the research is organized into four main sections: (i) a theoretical framework that places the SI alongside social democratic and market socialist traditions, highlighting tensions, convergences, and points of friction; (ii) an analytical framework that translates Situationist concepts into evaluative categories applicable to the study of concrete reforms; (iii) empirical case studies—the reduction of the working day in Iceland and cooperative development in Mondragón—that illustrate transformative possibilities and contextual limitations; and (iv) a critical synthesis that analyzes the scope and limits of so-called *non-reformist reforms*, proposing criteria to evaluate their capacity to open up spaces toward Situationist horizons (Gorz, 1967; Holloway, 2002; Debord, 1967).

Overall, the research seeks to offer an analytical perspective that combines empirical rigor, critical sensitivity, and a normatively ambitious vision: to show how institutional reforms can function as laboratories of social experimentation capable of articulating material emancipation, creativity, and political participation, without losing sight of the risks of neutralization, co-optation, and the reproduction of dominant capitalist logics.

1.1 What a Situationist Perspective Adds

This book does not merely revisit familiar debates on social democracy, market socialism, or progressive institutional reform. Its central contribution is to interrogate these traditions through a Situationist lens that foregrounds dimensions of social transformation often left implicit in political economy and institutional analysis. While much critical literature rightly emphasizes ownership structures, distributional outcomes, and macro-institutional design (Wright, 2010a; Schweickart, 2011a), Situationist theory insists that everyday life—time, activity, desire, and subjectivity—constitutes a decisive terrain of political struggle (Debord, 1994; Vaneigem, 2012).

From this perspective, reforms cannot be assessed solely in terms of efficiency, redistribution, or formal democratic control. The key question becomes whether they disrupt or reproduce what the Situationist International conceptualized as the *spectacle*: a historically specific form of social mediation in which social relations are organized through abstraction, separation, and passivity (Debord, 1994). Rather than treating the spectacle as an ideological overlay, the framework employed here understands it as a structuring condition of everyday experience, shaping how individuals encounter work, leisure, consumption, and political participation.

This emphasis distinguishes a Situationist critique from both classical Marxist and institutionalist approaches. Transformations in ownership or governance, while necessary, do not automatically translate into emancipatory forms of life. Capitalist domination operates not only through exploitation and exclusion but through the colonization of everyday practices, temporal structures, and forms of desire (Lefebvre, 1991a). The analytical task is therefore not to oppose institutional reform as such, but to distinguish between reforms that stabilize existing forms of alienation and those that plausibly alter the conditions of lived experience.

Accordingly, the Situationist framework functions in this book as a diagnostic and evaluative standard rather than as a comprehensive economic blueprint. It allows us to ask whether reforms such as work-time reduction, democratic ownership, universal basic income, or participatory urbanism merely redistribute resources within the same spectacular logic, or whether they expand lived autonomy, creative activity, and collective control over time and space. These questions shift the focus from formal institutional change alone to the experiential consequences of reform.

This approach also moves beyond the reform/revolution binary by treating out-comes as contingent rather than predetermined. Progressive reforms are neither inherently emancipatory nor inevitably recuperated. Their effects depend on political struggle, cultural embedding, and institutional design. Drawing on debates around co-optation, recuperation, and non-reformist reforms (Gorz, 1968; Boltanski and Chiapello, 2005), the book examines the conditions under which reforms may function as bridges toward qualitatively different forms of social life rather than as mechanisms of stabilization.

Finally, the Situationist perspective highlights the cultural and symbolic embedding of economic forms. Reforms operate not only through formal rules but through everyday practices, norms, and meanings. Whether policies such as universal basic income or workplace democracy enable autonomy or reproduce alienation depends on how they are framed, institutionalized, and lived. By complementing political economy with an analysis of everyday life, the book advances a framework for evaluating transformative potential that links institutional change to the reinvention of lived experience.

The chapters that follow operationalize this framework and apply it to concrete domains of reform. Rather than offering definitive prescriptions, the analysis develops criteria for assessing whether institutional transformations create conditions for temporal autonomy, unmediated social relations, creative praxis, and collective self-determination—dimensions that are essential for any project of post-capitalist transformation.

Conceptual Clarification: Capitalism, Markets, and Market Socialism

Throughout the book, it is important to distinguish analytically between capitalism, markets, and market socialism, terms that are often conflated in both scholarly and political debate. Capitalism is understood here not simply as the presence of markets, but as a specific configuration of social relations characterized by private ownership of productive assets, wage labor, profit-driven accumulation, and the subordination of social life to imperatives of valorization.

Markets, by contrast, refer to mechanisms of coordination and exchange. While historically intertwined with capitalism, markets are neither conceptually nor historically reducible to capitalist social relations, and may operate under a variety of ownership and institutional arrangements. Recognizing this distinction is particularly important when assessing proposals that seek to retain market coordination while transforming underlying relations of ownership and control. Market socialism encompasses a heterogeneous family of approaches that combine social or collective ownership with market-based allocation mechanisms. Some strands conceive market socialism as a reformist trajectory within capitalism, while others explicitly frame it as a systemic alternative involving a fundamental rupture with capitalist property relations. In this book, market socialist experiments are not treated as a unified model, but as empirical sites through which to examine the tensions between institutional change, everyday practices, and the persistence of commodified social relations.

This conceptual distinction allows the analysis to focus less on the formal presence or absence of markets, and more on whether specific institutional arrangements expand meaningful autonomy, collective control over time, and non-alienated forms of social activity—the core criteria emphasized by a Situationist perspective.

Also, throughout the book, references to social democracy should be understood not as a description of contemporary governing parties, but as shorthand for a historical repertoire of reformist strategies and policy instruments whose political carriers have substantially changed since the 1990s.

1.2 Book Roadmap

For ease of reading, the book is organized as follows:

- **Chapter 2: Theoretical Framework.** The conceptual basis of the work is established.

  - **Subsection 2.1: The Situationist International: Critique and Praxis.** This section explores the theory and practices of the SI, including a detailed analysis of the society of the spectacle, the revolution of everyday life, and the group's influence on events like May 1968.
  - **Subsection 2.2: Social Democracy: Reform within Capitalism.** This section presents the history and theory of social democracy, with a focus on its classic post-war model.

- **Chapter 3: Analytical Framework for Situationist Praxis.** A conceptual framework is presented that translates SI concepts into analytical categories for evaluating concrete reforms, such as decommodification and the reappropriation of time and space.
- **Chapter 4: Case Studies and Synthesis.** The analytical framework is applied to empirical case studies: the reduction of the working day in Iceland (4.1) and cooperative development in Mondragón (4.2). The section concludes with a synthesis that evaluates the scope and limits of 'non-reformist' reforms.
- **Chapter 5: Criticisms, Limitations, and Responses.** This chapter critically examines the main objections to the book's central argument, including the risks of co-optation and recuperation, limits to generalizability, tensions in translating Situationist theory to institutional analysis, and temporal and structural constraints on reform. Rather than treating these critiques as external refutations, the chapter engages them as constitutive tensions, developing a systematic response that clarifies the scope, ambitions, and strategic conditions under which social-democratic and market socialist reforms may open pathways toward a post-spectacular society.
- **Chapter 6: Conclusion and Future Discussion.** The main findings are summarized, reaffirming the argument that institutional reforms can generate the conditions for a post-spectacular society, and future lines of research are proposed.

CHAPTER 2

Theoretical Framework

2.1 The Situationist International: Critique and Praxis

The Situationist International emerged from the convergence of avant-garde art movements and revolutionary Marxist critique in post-war Europe. Founded in 1957 through the merger of groups like the Lettrist International, the International Movement for an Imaginist Bauhaus, and COBRA, the SI represented a unique synthesis of aesthetic experimentation and political radicalism (Marcus, 1989; McDowell, 2004). This convergence was not merely organizational; it involved a fundamental reconceptualization of the relationship between art and politics, rejecting both the autonomy of art and the instrumentalization of culture for narrow political ends.

The historical context of the SI's emergence cannot be underestimated. Postwar reconstruction generated unprecedented material prosperity in Western Europe, but at the same time, it was marked by new forms of alienation and social control. The rise of consumer capitalism, the expansion of bureaucratic institutions, and the appearance of mass media created conditions that traditional Marxist analysis seemed unable to address. The SI's intervention sought to close this analytical gap by extending critical theory to domains previously considered peripheral to revolutionary politics.

M. Brum, *Democratic Alternatives*,
https://doi.org/10.1007/978-3-032-23153-6_2

The intellectual genealogy of the SI can be traced through multiple traditions: the Dadaist critique of bourgeois culture, the Surrealist exploration of unconscious desire, the architectural radicalism of the modern movement, and the heterodox Marxism of figures like Henri Lefebvre and György Lukács (Lefebvre, 1991b; Lukács, 1971). This synthetic approach allowed the SI to develop a critique of capitalism that was simultaneously structural and phenomenological, systemic and experiential.

2.1.1 *The Society of the Spectacle: Theoretical Foundations and Implications*

La Société du Spectacle (1967) by Guy Debord constituted the fundamental theoretical contribution of the SI, offering a comprehensive analysis of advanced capitalist society that extended Marx's critique of political into the realm of culture and everyday experience (Debord, 1967). Debord argued that, in advanced capitalism, social relationships are increasingly mediated by representations, images, and commodities, creating a totalizing system of domination that he called the "spectacle."

The spectacle is not merely a collection of media images or propaganda; it constitutes a fundamental transformation in the very organization of social life. As Debord famously formulated in his thesis: "The spectacle is not a collection of images, but a social relationship among people, mediated by images" (Debord, 1967, thesis 4). This definition reveals the dialectical nature of the spectacle: it is simultaneously material and ideological, structural and phenomenological.

Debord's analysis expands upon Marx's ideas on commodity fetishism and Georg Lukács's theory of reification to encompass the totality of social experience (Marx, 1976; Lukács, 1971). While Marx focused primarily on the mystification of social relations through commodity exchange, and Lukács examined the rationalization of consciousness under capitalism, Debord argued that the spectacle represents the culmination of these processes. In spectacular society, the commodity form becomes the organizing principle not only of production and exchange but of perception, desire, and social interaction itself.

This theoretical framework allowed the SI to analyze phenomena that traditional Marxism had difficulty addressing: the role of mass media in shaping consciousness, the transformation of politics into spectacle, the commodification of leisure and culture, and the emergence of what would later be called "lifestyle" as a form of identity. The spectacle transforms individuals into passive consumers of prefabricated experiences, eroding their capacity for autonomous, creative, and collective action.

The concept of spectacular accumulation provides a crucial bridge between classical political economy and cultural critique. Debord argued that the spectacle represents a new phase of capitalist development, in which the production of images, experiences, and subjectivities becomes central to accumulation strategies (Debord, 1970). This perspective anticipated later developments in critical theory, including the analysis of "immaterial labor" and the "experience economy" (Lazzarato, 1996; Pine and Gilmore, 1999).

Debord's critique resonated with broader developments in critical theory, particularly the Frankfurt School's analysis of the "culture industry" and Herbert Marcuse's concept of the "one-dimensional man" (Adorno and Horkheimer, 2002; Marcuse, 1969). However, the distinctive contribution of the SI resided in its emphasis on totality: the spectacle was not simply ideological domination but a comprehensive reorganization of social relations that required an equally comprehensive revolutionary response.

The geographical and temporal dimensions of the spectacle also deserve attention. Debord analyzed how spectacular society transforms space into a series of commodified zones while simultaneously compressing historical time into an eternal present of consumption. This spatiotemporal analysis influenced later work in critical geography and cultural studies, particularly David Harvey's analysis of timespace compression and Henri Lefebvre's work on the production of space (Harvey, 1989; Lefebvre, 1991b).

2.1.2 *The Revolution of Everyday Life: Subjectivity and Liberation*

Traité de savoir-vivre à l'usage des jeunes générations (1967) by Raoul Vaneigem, translated as *The Revolution of Everyday Life*, complemented Debord's systemic analysis with an emphasis on subjectivity, desire, and lived experience (Vaneigem, 1967). While Debord's analysis remained relatively abstract and structural, Vaneigem's work explored the phenomenology of alienation and the possibilities of overcoming it at the level of immediate experience.

Vaneigem argued that revolutionary transformation should not be limited to dismantling capitalist institutions but should also liberate the everyday from bureaucratic control, alienated labor, and commodified leisure. This perspective represented a significant expansion of traditional revolutionary theory, which had typically focused on seizing state power or controlling the means of production. For Vaneigem, the colonization of everyday life by capital and bureaucracy required liberation strategies that operated at the micropolitical level of daily experience.

Central to Vaneigem's analysis was the concept of "survival," which he clearly distinguished from authentic life. Under spectacular capitalism, individuals are reduced to mere survival: the reproduction of life as abstract labor power, rather than the creative realization of human potential. This reduction operates through multiple mechanisms: the separation of work and play, the commodification of desire, the bureaucratization of social interaction, and the transformation of life into a series of predetermined roles and functions.

The revolutionary potential of everyday life lay precisely in its condition as a space where these mechanisms of domination could be most directly challenged. Vaneigem emphasized the importance of moments of authentic experience—what the SI called "situations"—to reveal the poverty of existing social arrangements and point toward alternative possibilities. These moments could arise spontaneously in love, play, festivity, or revolt, but they could also be consciously constructed through Situationist practices.

Vaneigem's emphasis on subjectivity and desire drew on earlier critiques of industrial civilization, particularly those of Charles Fourier and the Surrealists, while anticipating later feminist insights on the political dimensions of domestic life and emotional labor (Fourier, 1996; Federici, 2012). His work also prefigured developments in anti-psychiatry, especially the critique of the normalization and pathologization of deviance (Laing, 1967; Deleuze and Guattari, 1977).

The relationship between individual liberation and collective transformation posed complex theoretical and practical questions for the SI. Vaneigem rejected both individualist solutions that ignored structural constraints and collectivist approaches that subsumed individuality into abstract social categories. Instead, he sought to theorize a form of revolutionary subjectivity that was simultaneously personal and political, individual and collective.

This approach influenced later movements that sought to bridge the gap between personal and political transformation, including second-wave feminism, the environmental movement, and various forms of cultural politics. The slogan "the personal is political" can be understood as a popularization of ideas initially developed within Situationist theory (Hanisch, 1970).

The dialectical unity between Debord's structural critique and Vaneigem's emphasis on subjectivity encapsulates the SI's distinctive approach: neither purely objectivist nor subjectivist, but centered on the lived totality of capitalist domination and the possibilities for its revolutionary overcoming.

2.1.3 Situationist Practices: Theory in Action

The SI articulated its politics through experimental practices rather than conventional organization, developing a repertoire of techniques aimed at disrupting spectacular relations and generating possibilities for authentic experience. Two concepts proved particularly influential and enduring: *dérive* and *détournement*.

The *dérive*, or "drift," was an experimental urban wandering designed to subvert functionalist urban planning and reveal new spatial possibilities (Debord, 1956). This practice arose from the SI's critique of modern urbanism, particularly the functionalist planning principles associated with Le Corbusier and the Bauhaus, which divided cities into rational zones for work, residence, and consumption. The *dérive* sought to rediscover the city as a space of encounter, play, and possibility, rather than a space of efficient circulation and productive activity.

The theoretical foundations of the *dérive* were based on multiple sources: the surrealist practice of automatic wandering, the anthropological concept of psychogeography, and the architectural theory of "unitary urbanism." Psychogeography, defined as "the study of the precise laws and specific effects of the geographical environment on the emotions and behavior of individuals," provided a framework for understanding how spatial arrangements shape consciousness and social relations (Debord, 1955).

In practice, the *dérive* involved small groups of two or three people who abandoned their usual activities and motives for movement through the city, allowing themselves to be drawn by the terrain's attractions and the encounters that occurred there. This practice generated new knowledge about urban space, while also creating moments of authentic experience that sharply contrasted with the instrumental use of space characteristic of spectacular society.

The political implications of the *dérive* extended beyond urban planning, en-compassing broader questions of social organization. By revealing the constructed nature of seemingly natural spatial arrangements, the practice demonstrated the possibility of alternative forms of urban life. This perspective influenced later movements in critical urban theory, tactical urbanism, and the right to the city (Harvey, 2012; Lefebvre, 1996).

Détournement consisted of the appropriation and subversion of existing cultural forms—advertisements, comic strips, political slogans, newspaper headlines—to expose their ideological function and redirect them toward revolutionary ends (Debord & Wolman, 1956). This technique embodied the SI's analysis of spectacular society as a system of communication and representation, rather than simply as economic exploitation.

The practice of *détournement* operated on multiple levels simultaneously. On the most immediate level, it provided a means of communication that could reach audiences beyond the traditional Left, bypassing the commodified channels of spectacular media. More fundamentally, *détournement* demonstrated the constructed nature of seemingly natural cultural forms, revealing their ideological content and opening up space for alternative meanings.

Theoretically, *détournement* was based on Walter Benjamin's concept of montage and Bertolt Brecht's alienation effect techniques, anticipating later practices such as culture jamming, media activism, and remix culture (Benjamin, 1968a; Brecht, 1964). The technique also reflected the understanding of revolutionary theory itself as a form of *détournement*: the appropriation and transformation of existing theoretical materials for new purposes.

The political effectiveness of *détournement* resided in its ability to operate within spectacular communication channels while subverting their intended effects. This approach offered an alternative both to the traditional Left's reliance on counterinstitutional media and the avant-garde's retreat into aesthetic autonomy.

Other Situationist practices included the construction of situations, the exploration of constructed situations, and the development of unitary urbanism. The construction of situations involved the conscious creation of environments conducive to authentic experience and genuine encounter. This practice required careful attention to spatial arrangement, temporal rhythms, and social dynamics to generate conditions that would facilitate the emergence of new forms of behavior and relationships (Kotanyi & Vaneigem, 1961).

These practices illustrate the SI's broader methodological approach: instead of proposing alternative institutions or engaging in conventional political organizing, the Situationists sought to create moments of authentic experience that would reveal the poverty of existing social arrangements and point toward revolutionary possibilities. This approach reflected their understanding of revolution as a qualitative transformation of everyday life, rather than a simple change in political leadership or economic ownership.

2.1.4 Political Positions and Strategic Orientations

Politically, the SI maintained an uncompromising rejection of reformism, parliamentary politics, and traditional labor organizations, considering them complicit in the reproduction of spectacular relations rather than their challenge (Viénet, 1968). This stance reflected both anarchist influences and a heterodox Marxist critique of actually existing socialism, understood as another form of bureaucratic domination and spectacular representation.

The SI's critique of traditional left-wing politics operated on several levels. First, they argued that parliamentary politics and union organization perpetuated the separation between political representation and direct participation, characteristic of spectacular society. By channeling popular energy into institutionalized forms, these practices prevented the emergence of genuinely revolutionary consciousness and activity.

Second, the SI analyzed both Western social democracy and Eastern European socialism as variants of the same spectacular system, differing only in their specific mechanisms of domination and mystification. In both cases, bureaucratic elites managed populations through a combination of material concessions and ideological manipulation, preventing the emergence of genuine self-organization and autonomous activity.

This analysis led the SI to advocate for a form of revolutionary politics they called "council communism," drawing inspiration from the tradition of workers' councils that emerged during revolutionary periods in Russia, Germany, and Hungary (Pannekoek, 1948). However, the SI extended this concept beyond labor organization to encompass all aspects of social life, advocating for the creation of situations that prefigured revolutionary society rather than merely opposing existing institutions.

The SI's relationship with other radical movements of the 1960s was complex and often antagonistic. Although they shared certain critiques with the New Left, especially regarding bureaucracy and authoritarianism, the SI rejected what it considered reformist tendencies and the spectacular recuperation of movements like Students for a Democratic Society and various national liberation movements (Vaneigem, 1974).

The SI's analysis of recuperation—the process by which spectacular society absorbs and neutralizes potentially subversive forces—led them to maintain a critical distance from mass movements that could compromise the radical character of Situationist theory and practice. This stance often put them at odds with other left-wing groups and contributed to their reputation for sectarian behavior.

2.1.5 May 1968: Theory in Practice

The events of May 1968 in France constituted the historical moment when the SI's influence became most visible and its ideas received their most dramatic practical confirmation (Ross, 2002). Although the SI's direct organizational role in May 1968 remains debated, their ideas clearly influenced both the cultural dimensions of the revolt and its critique of consumer society.

The uprising began with student protests at the University of Nanterre but quickly spread beyond the educational system to encompass a general critique of French society. Slogans like "Sous les pavés, la plage!" (Under the cobblestones, the beach!), "Il est interdit d'interdire" (It is forbidden to forbid), and "L'imagination au pouvoir" (All power to the imagination!) captured the Situationist spirit of reclaiming life from commodification and bureaucratic control.

The SI's analysis of the society of the spectacle provided a framework for understanding why the revolt took the form it did. Rather than focusing exclusively on economic demands or political representation, the movement questioned the totality of social relations under advanced capitalism. Students rejected not only authoritarian pedagogy but the entire educational apparatus as a mechanism for producing passive consumers and compliant workers.

The occupation of factories by workers represented a further extension of Situationist insights into the sphere of production. Instead of solely demanding higher wages or better working conditions, workers began to question the very nature of work and to experiment with new forms of organization and decision-making. This prefigured later developments in autonomist Marxism and the critique of work (Cleaver, 1979; Weeks, 2011).

The cultural dimensions of May 1968—the proliferation of posters, graffiti, and slogans; the transformation of public space into a forum for debate and encounter; the explosion of creative activity and festive behavior—demonstrated the practical relevance of Situationist concepts like the construction of situations and the revolution of everyday life.

However, the eventual recuperation of May 1968—its transformation into a spectacle of youthful rebellion and cultural modernization—also confirmed the SI's analysis of spectacular society's ability to absorb and neutralize potentially subversive forces. The events that began as a radical critique consumer capitalism ultimately contributed to the further development of this system, as the movement's cultural innovations were commodified and sold back to their creators.

2.1.6 Dissolution and Legacy

The SI dissolved in 1972, in part due to internal conflicts over the relationship between theory and practice, and also because of broader strategic disagreements about how to respond to the recuperation of May 1968 (Hussey, 2001). Some members advocated for a greater engagement with mass movements and practical organization, while others insisted on maintaining the purity of Situationist theory in the face of spectacular contamination.

These internal tensions reflected deeper theoretical problems within Situationist theory itself. The emphasis on authentic experience and the construction of situations generated difficulties in developing sustainable forms of political organization and practice. The critique of representation made it hard to elaborate strategies for engaging broader populations, while the rejection of programmatic politics created problems for articulating concrete alternatives to existing institutions.

Despite these limitations, the intellectual legacy of the SI persisted and expanded in multiple directions. Autonomist Marxism, particularly the work of Mario Tronti, Antonio Negri, and Franco Berardi, developed Situationist insights on the transformation of capitalist production and the role of subjectivity in contemporary capitalism (Hardt & Negri, 2000; Berardi, 2009).

Critical urban theory, especially the works of Henri Lefebvre, David Harvey, and Neil Smith, extended the Situationist analysis of space and urbanization into systematic critiques of capitalist urbanization and the production of space (Lefebvre, 1991b; Harvey, 2012; Smith, 1984).

Cultural studies and media theory incorporated Situationist insights on spectacular representation and cultural politics, influencing work on ideology, popular culture, and media activism (Kellner, 2003; Best and Kellner, 1997). The concept of *détournement* proved particularly influential in the development of culture jamming, tactical media, and various forms of media activism.

Contemporary social movements have widely drawn on Situationist theory and practice, especially in their emphasis on prefigurative politics, the critique of representation, and the transformation of everyday life. The alter-globalization movement, Occupy Wall Street, and various forms of urban activism have incorporated Situationist ideas, adapting them to current conditions (Graeber, 2009; Mason, 2012).

The environmental movement has found particular resonance with the Situationist critiques of industrial capitalism and consumer society, while feminist theory has developed Situationist insights on the politics of everyday life and the personal dimensions of political transformation (Merchant, 1980; Federici, 2012).

However, the recuperation of Situationist ideas in academic discourse and artistic practice also demonstrates the continuing relevance of the SI's analysis of the spectacular society. The transformation of radical critique into academic capital and cultural commodity confirms their observations on the spectacular society's ability to absorb and neutralize potentially subversive forces.

The contemporary relevance of Situationist theory does not lie in its specific prescriptions or practices, but in its systematic critique of the colonization of everyday life by capital and its insistence on the revolutionary potential of authentic experience and genuine encounter. In an era of social media, surveillance capitalism, and the commodification of previously intimate domains of human experience, the Situationist analysis of the spectacular society becomes increasingly insightful and necessary (Zuboff, 2019; Srnicek, 2017).

2.2 Social Democracy: Reform Within Capitalism

Social democracy emerged in the late nineteenth century in Europe as the political expression of socialist movements that sought workers' empowerment through parliamentary means rather than revolutionary transformations (Sassoon, 1996). This reformist orientation distinguished social democrats both from revolutionary Marxists and from liberal politicians, positioning them as advocates for gradual socialist transformation through democratic institutions and state intervention in market economies.

The intellectual foundations of social democracy can be traced back to the revisionist debates within European Marxism, particularly Eduard Bernstein's influential critique of orthodox Marxist revolutionary theory (Bernstein, 1899). Bernstein argued that Marx's predictions about capitalist crisis and immiseration had been proven incorrect, and that socialism could be achieved through gradual reforms rather than revolutionary ruptures. This theoretical shift allowed social democratic parties to participate in bourgeois parliamentary systems while maintaining their commitment to socialist transformation.

The institutional development of social democracy reflected broader transformations in capitalist societies, particularly the extension of suffrage, the organization of industrial working classes, and the expansion of state capacity. Social democratic parties like the German SPD, the British Labour Party, and the Swedish SAP emerged as mass organizations capable of mobilizing working-class voters and implementing reformist policies through democratic processes (Przeworski, 1985).

In its classic post-war form, particularly between 1945 and the mid-1970s, social democracy represented a historical compromise between capital and labor that fundamentally altered the character of capitalist societies. This compromise was facilitated by specific historical conditions: the devastation of the Second World War, Cold War competition with Soviet socialism, rapid economic growth, and the organizational strength of labor movements (Maier, 1987).

The theoretical framework of post-war social democracy synthesized multiple intellectual traditions: Keynesian economic theory offered tools for macroeconomic management; Fabian socialism proposed models for gradual institutional reform; Christian social doctrine contributed notions of social solidarity; and liberal-democratic theory provided frameworks for political participation and individual rights (Jackson, 2007).

2.2.1 *The Golden Age Model: Institutional Architecture and Social Outcomes*

Post-war social democracy combined Keynesian demand management, full employment policies, progressive taxation, expansive welfare states, and corporatist bargaining structures into a coherent institutional framework that fundamentally transformed the relationship between state, market, and society (Esping-Andersen, 1990). This model achieved unprecedented levels of social security, reduced inequality, and created conditions for mass social mobility in Western Europe while maintaining capitalist property relations and market allocation mechanisms (Judt, 2005).

The Keynesian dimension of social democracy involved state management of aggregate demand through fiscal and monetary policies to maintain full employment and stable growth. This represented a fundamental departure from classical liberal economics, which assumed that markets are self-regulating and that unemployment resulted from wage rigidities rather than insufficient demand (Keynes, 1936). Social democratic governments used deficit spending, public investment, and countercyclical policies to stabilize economic fluctuations and maintain high levels of employment.

The welfare state component involved the creation of comprehensive systems of social insurance, public services, and income support that provided citizens with security against market risks and life contingencies (Marshall, 1950). These institutions went beyond poverty relief, establishing new forms of social citizenship that guaranteed access to healthcare, education, housing, and income security as rights, not as charity.

Progressive taxation systems ensured that the costs of welfare provision were distributed according to ability to pay, also serving redistributive functions that reduced post-tax inequality. Top marginal rates reached between 80–90% in some countries during the 1960s and 1970s, allowing for a substantial redistribution from capital to labor and from high to low incomes (Piketty, 2014).

Corporatist bargaining structures institutionalized cooperation among employers, unions, and governments in wage setting, economic planning, and social policy development (Katzenstein, 1985). These agreements allowed social democratic governments to coordinate macroeconomic policy with wage moderation and industrial relations, creating conditions for sustained growth with low inflation.

The social democratic welfare state transcended mere redistribution, embodying a vision of citizenship and decommodification that challenged the logic of market society. Gøsta Esping-Andersen's influential typology conceptualized welfare regimes as mechanisms that "decommodify" labor, allowing individuals to maintain livelihoods independent of the market (Esping-Andersen, 1990). Universal healthcare, education, pensions, and unemployment insurance created spheres of social life protected from market logic, allowing citizens to make decisions about work, family, and personal development without facing destitution.

The concept of decommodification was particularly important for understanding the transformative potential of social democratic institutions. By reducing the necessity for individuals to sell their labor power to survive, welfare states created conditions for greater autonomy, creativity, and solidarity. Workers could resist exploitative employers, women could reduce their dependence on male providers, and families could invest in education and care without facing economic insecurity.

Nordic social democracy represented the most developed version of this model, combining high taxation, generous social benefits, and active employment policies with strong economic performance and social cohesion (Pontusson, 2011). The "Swedish model" became synonymous with the possibility of combining economic efficiency with social equality through institutional innovation, demonstrating that redistributive policies do not necessarily undermine economic dynamism.

The Swedish case illustrated several key features of successful social democracy: universal welfare policies that generated broad coalitions of support; active labor market policies that facilitated economic restructuring while protecting workers; wage solidarity policies that compressed income inequality; and democratic participation in economic planning through tripartite institutions (Korpi, 1983).

Beyond the Nordic countries, social democratic achievements varied considerably according to national contexts. The British welfare state emphasized universalism in health and education while maintaining more limited income supports; French social democracy combined extensive social insurance with dirigiste economic planning; German social democracy created comprehensive social insurance systems within a federal framework; and Austrian social democracy developed distinctive forms of social partnership and industrial nationalization (Castles, 1978).

The economic outcomes of social democratic governance during the Golden Age were remarkable: Western Europe achieved sustained full employment, with unemployment rates typically below 3% between 1945 and 1975. Income inequality decreased sharply, with Gini coefficients dropping from pre-war levels of 0.5–0.6 to post-war levels of 0.2–0.3 in many countries. Social mobility increased significantly, as working-class children gained access to higher education and professional careers through meritocratic selection and public investment in education (Therborn, 1995). The social and cultural transformations associated with social democracy were equally significant. The expansion of public education created a more informed and engaged citizenry; universal healthcare improved population health and reduced health inequalities; public housing programs provided decent accommodation for working families; and cultural policies supported the arts, libraries, and public broadcasting (Wagner, 1990).

Gender relations were deeply affected by social democratic institutions, though often in contradictory ways. On one hand, public services and social benefits reduced women's dependence on male providers and created new employment opportunities; on the other, social democratic policies reinforced traditional gender roles by supporting male industrial employment and treating women primarily as mothers and caregivers (Lewis, 1992).

The international dimensions of social democratic success cannot be ignored. The Bretton Woods system provided stable exchange rates and capital controls that enabled national economic management; the Cold War incentivized Western governments to demonstrate the superiority of democratic capitalism over Soviet socialism; and rapid economic growth provided resources for welfare state expansion without threatening capitalist accumulation (Ruggie, 1982).

2.2.2 Critiques and Contradictions: Theoretical and Practical Challenges

Social democracy faced sustained critiques from both Marxist and neoliberal perspectives, which identified fundamental contradictions within the social democratic project that would ultimately contribute to its crisis and transformation. These critiques operated on multiple levels: theoretical analyses of the structural limitations of reform within capitalism, empirical studies of the contradictions of the welfare state, and political challenges to social democratic hegemony.

Marxist scholars developed sophisticated analyses of the structural constraints facing social democratic policy. Claus Offe argued that welfare institutions remain fundamentally limited by the imperatives of capitalist accumulation, generating systematic contradictions between the needs of legitimation and the requirements of profitability (Offe, 1984). The welfare state can stabilize capitalism by mitigating its worst effects, rather than transcending capitalist social relations, creating what Offe termed the "crisis of crisis management."

According to this analysis, social democratic policies face a double bind: they must provide enough benefits to maintain political legitimacy and social cohesion, but they cannot redistribute so much as to undermine profitability and capitalist investment. This structural limitation means that welfare states tend to oscillate between periods of expansion and retrenchment, unable to achieve stable solutions to the contradictions of capitalist development.

James O'Connor's analysis of the "fiscal crisis of the state" was another influential Marxist critique of social democracy (O'Connor, 1973). O'Connor argued that capitalist states face contradictory imperatives to support both accumulation (profitable private investment) and legitimation (social cohesion and political stability). The costs of fulfilling both functions tend to grow faster than the tax base, generating chronic fiscal crises that force governments to choose between supporting capital or popular welfare.

Neo-Marxist regulation theorists like Michel Aglietta and Alain Lipietz analyzed social democracy as a particular form of capitalist regulation that temporarily resolved the contradictions of capitalist development through Keynesian-Fordist institutions (Aglietta, 1979; Lipietz, 1987). However, they argued that this regulatory framework contained internal contradictions that would eventually undermine its effectiveness, leading to a crisis and the emergence of new forms of capitalist regulation.

The feminist critique of social democracy highlighted its gendered nature and its role in reproducing patriarchal relations within the welfare state. Scholars like Carole Pateman and Nancy Fraser argued that social democratic citizenship remained fundamentally masculine, based on the model of the male industrial worker, while women were relegated to a dependent status as wives and mothers (Pateman, 1988; Fraser, 1994). The social democratic welfare state thus institutionalized gender inequality even while promoting class equality.

From the right, neoliberal economists developed systematic critiques of social democratic policies as economically inefficient and politically dangerous. Friedrich Hayek argued that social democratic planning and redistribution undermined the price mechanism that coordinates complex modern economies, leading inevitably to economic decline and political authoritarianism (Hayek, 1944). This critique positioned social democracy as a step on the "road to serfdom," which would ultimately destroy both prosperity and liberty.

Milton Friedman and other Chicago School economists offered more technical critiques of specific social democratic policies. They argued that minimum wage laws created unemployment by pricing low-skilled workers out of the labor market; that progressive taxation reduced incentives to work, save, and invest; that public monopolies in health and education were less efficient than market provision; and that Keynesian demand management generated inflation without reducing structural unemployment (Friedman, 1962).

Public choice theorists like James Buchanan and Gordon Tullock analyzed social democratic politics as a form of rent-seeking that allowed special interests to appropriate resources from productive economic actors (Buchanan and Tullock, 1962). According to this analysis, democratic politics systematically favors concentrated interests (like public sector unions) over diffuse interests (like taxpayers), leading to excessive government growth and a decline in economic performance.

The stagflation crisis of the 1970s provided empirical evidence for the neoliberal critiques, as social democratic countries experienced simultaneous inflation and unemployment, something that Keynesian theory suggested was impossible. This crisis undermined confidence in social democratic economic management and created opportunities for neoliberal politicians like Margaret Thatcher and Ronald Reagan to implement alternative policies (Krugman, 2009).

The neoliberal offensive initiated in the 1980s subjected welfare institutions to systematic cuts, privatization, and austerity across much of Europe and North America (Harvey, 2005). This process included multiple strategies: direct cuts to benefits and public services; privatization of public enterprises and services; deregulation of financial and labor markets; tax cuts that diminished government revenues; and the creation of institutional frameworks that limited public spending and monetary policy.

While social democratic parties adapted to these neoliberal constraints, often adopting "Third Way" policies that accepted market mechanisms while attempting to mitigate their social consequences, the original social democratic compromise seemed increasingly anachronistic (Giddens, 1998). Third Way social democracy abandoned commitments to full employment, accepted greater inequality as the price of economic flexibility, and shifted from universal welfare provision toward targeted assistance to the most disadvantaged.

The process of European integration created additional constraints for social democratic policy by establishing supranational institutions committed to market liberalization and fiscal orthodoxy. The European Union's competition policy limited state intervention in the economy, while the European Monetary Union imposed fiscal restrictions that prevented countercyclical spending (Streeck, 2014). These developments reduced the policy space available to social democratic governments and contributed to the convergence of center-left and center-right economic policies.

Globalization posed additional challenges to social democratic policy by increasing capital mobility, intensifying international competition, and reducing the effectiveness of national economic policies. The threat of capital flight limited redistributive policies, while international tax competition reduced government revenues. Social democratic parties found themselves competing to attract mobile capital through corporate tax cuts, labor deregulation, and cuts to public spending (Scharpf, 1999).

2.2.3 *Internal Contradictions and Sociological Transformations*

Beyond external critiques, social democracy faced internal contradictions arising from its own success. The expansion of higher education and public sector employment created new middle-class constituencies with different interests from traditional industrial workers. These "new class" professionals often supported cultural liberalization and environmental protection but were ambivalent about redistributive policies that primarily benefited working-class voters (Bell, 1973).

The decline of industrial employment and the growth of service sectors fragmented the working class and weakened union organization. Private sector workers faced greater job insecurity and wage stagnation, while those in the public sector enjoyed greater security and benefits, creating tensions within social democratic electoral coalitions (Kitschelt, 1994).

Immigration and multiculturalism posed additional challenges to social democratic solidarity by introducing cultural diversity into previously homogenous societies. Research in social psychology suggests that ethnic diversity can weaken support for redistributive policies by eroding in-group solidarity and trust (Putnam, 2007). Right-wing populist parties exploited these tensions by combining anti-immigrant rhetoric with a defense of welfare programs for native citizens.

Generational replacement of voters also affected social democratic politics. Younger voters, who grew up with the protections of the welfare state, took them for granted, showing greater concern for post-material issues such as environmental protection, gender equality, and cultural diversity. This shift in political priorities reduced support for traditional social democratic concerns about class inequality and industrial relations (Inglehart, 1997).

2.2.4 *Contemporary Relevance and Renewal*

Despite these challenges, social democratic ideas have experienced renewed interest amid rising inequality, the climate crisis, and the limitations of neoliberal governance. Contemporary proposals like universal basic income, the reduction of the working day, Green New Deal policies, and the regulation of digital platforms are explicitly inspired by social democratic traditions, adapting them to current conditions (Standing, 2017; Jackson, 2017).

The COVID-19 pandemic offered a dramatic demonstration of the continuing relevance of social democratic principles, as governments worldwide implemented emergency measures—furlough schemes, expanded unemployment benefits, investments in public health, industrial policies—that were reminiscent of classic social democratic policies (Mazzucato, 2020). The rapid mobilization of state resources to address the health and economic crisis revealed the limitations of purely market-based approaches and the continuing importance of public sector capacity.

Climate change has created new imperatives for state intervention in the economy that evoke social democratic approaches to economic planning and industrial policy. Green New Deal proposals developed in the United States and Europe combine environmental protection with job creation, industrial transformation, and social justice in ways that recall the comprehensive approach of post-war social democracy (Pettifor, 2019).

The rise of inequality in advanced capitalist countries has renewed interest in redistributive policies and wealth taxes. Economists like Thomas Piketty have argued that contemporary levels of inequality are unsustainable and require new forms of progressive taxation and wealth redistribution (Piketty, 2014). Proposals like wealth taxes, inheritance taxes, and global fiscal coordination are inspired by social democratic traditions while confronting the challenges of globalized capitalism.

The digital revolution has generated new challenges and opportunities for social democratic politics. Platform capitalism has generated new forms of inequality and insecurity that require regulatory responses, while digital technologies offer possibilities for economic planning and democratic participation that could revitalize social democratic governance (Srnicek, 2017). Proposals for public digital platforms, data commons, and algorithmic accountability reflect attempts to apply social democratic principles to digital capitalism.

Contemporary social democratic parties have experimented with various strategies of renewal, including: embracing post-growth economics and degrowth policies; developing new forms of economic democracy through cooperatives and participatory budgeting; supporting universal basic services instead of universal basic income; and creating new forms of international cooperation to constrain global capitalism (Buch-Hansen, 2021).

The COVID-19 pandemic also demonstrated the continued importance of universalist welfare policies and public services. Countries with stronger public health systems and more generous unemployment benefits were better able to respond to the crisis while maintaining social cohesion. This experience reinforced arguments in favor of universal healthcare, public drug development, and robust welfare systems (Bambra, 2021).

2.2.5 *Theoretical Debates and Future Directions*

Contemporary social democratic theory faces several fundamental questions about the future of reform within capitalism. The first concerns whether traditional social democratic policies remain viable under conditions of globalized and financialized capitalism, or if new institutional frameworks are required to constrain capital mobility and restore national policy autonomy.

The second question involves the relationship between economic growth and environmental sustainability. Traditional social democracy assumed that economic growth could finance the expansion of the welfare state while improving living standards. However, climate change and environmental degradation raise questions about whether continued growth is compatible with planetary limits, leading some social democrats to embrace post-growth or degrowth policies (Jackson, 2017).

The third question concerns the institutional framework for democratic participation in complex, technologically mediated societies. Traditional social democracy relied on mass parties, trade unions, and representative institutions that may be inadequate for contemporary challenges. New forms of participatory, deliberative, and digital democracy offer potential alternatives to revitalize social democratic governance (Pateman, 2012).

The fourth question involves the scale of political organization needed to address global challenges like climate change, tax evasion, and technological disruption. National social democratic policies may be insufficient for problems that transcend borders, leading to calls for a European, global, or cosmopolitan social democracy (Held, 2004).

These debates reflect broader uncertainties about the future of capitalism and democracy in the twenty-first century. The continuing relevance of social democracy depends on its ability to adapt its institutional innovations and normative commitments to contemporary conditions, while maintaining its core: combining economic efficiency with social solidarity through democratic governance.

2.3 Market Socialism: Beyond Capitalist Property

Market socialism represents a distinct strand of socialist thought that seeks to transcend capitalism while preserving the allocative benefits and efficiency mechanisms of market coordination. Unlike social democracy, which accepts private property while regulating markets, market socialism envisions a fundamental transformation of property structures combined with competitive allocation mechanisms that retain the informational and incentive advantages of market systems, while eliminating capitalist exploitation and inequality (Roemer, 1994b).

The theoretical foundation of market socialism rests on the idea that the primary source of inequality and exploitation under capitalism resides not in market exchange per se, but in the private ownership of productive assets and the resulting capacity of capital owners to extract surplus value from workers. By socializing ownership while maintaining competitive markets, market socialists argue that it is possible to achieve both economic efficiency and distributive justice (Miller, 1989).

This approach distinguishes market socialism from both capitalist market systems and traditional centrally planned socialist economies. Market socialists reject the capitalist claim that private property is necessary for economic efficiency, while critiquing centrally planned socialism for its informational deficits, bureaucratic rigidities, and democratic deficits. The market socialist synthesis seeks to combine the dynamic efficiency of market competition with the egalitarian aspirations of socialist ownership (Bardhan & Roemer, 1993).

The intellectual development of market socialism reflects broader tensions within socialist theory between efficiency and equality, centralization and decentralization, planning and spontaneity. These tensions have generated diverse models of market socialism that vary in their approaches to property structures, market regulation, investment coordination, and democratic governance. Contemporary market socialist theory draws from multiple intellectual traditions: neoclassical economics to analyze market efficiency; Marxian political economy to study exploitation and class relations; participatory democratic theory for models of labor governance; and ecological economics to understand environmental constraints (Schweickart, 2011a).

The emergence of new technologies, particularly digital platforms and artificial intelligence, has created both opportunities and challenges for market socialist theorists. Digital technologies allow for new forms of coordination and participation that could facilitate democratic economic planning, while platform monopolies and surveillance capitalism display new forms of exploitation that require socialist responses (Fuchs, 2014).

2.3.1 Historical Development: From Calculation Debates to Democratic Models

The intellectual lineage of market socialism traces back to the famous interwar debates over the "socialist calculation problem," which fundamentally shaped 20thcentury economic theory. When Ludwig von Mises and Friedrich Hayek argued that rational economic calculation was impossible without private property and market prices, socialist economists like Oskar Lange, Abba Lerner, and Fred Taylor responded by proposing "market socialist" models that combined state ownership with simulated market mechanisms (Lange & Taylor, 1938; Mises, 1920; Hayek, 1945).

The original challenge from Mises, articulated in his 1920 essay "Economic Calculation in the Socialist Commonwealth," argued that without private ownership of capital goods and the market prices that arise from competitive exchange, socialist planners would lack the information necessary to allocate resources efficiently. This critique went to the heart of socialist planning theory by suggesting that the elimination of private property would necessarily result in economic irrationality and waste (Mises, 1920).

Hayek later developed this argument by emphasizing the dispersed character of economic knowledge and the impossibility of centralizing the tacit and contextual information that market prices automatically coordinate. The "knowledge problem" became a central concern for socialist theorists who sought to demonstrate the feasibility of non-capitalist economic organization (Hayek, 1945).

The socialist response, led by Oskar Lange and Abba Lerner, proposed market socialist models in which state-owned firms used accounting prices set by central planners to simulate market coordination. Lange's model involved a trial-and-error process in which planners adjusted prices based on indicators of surplus or shortage, eventually reaching equilibrium prices that would guide the efficient allocation of resources (Lange & Taylor, 1938).

While these early models demonstrated the theoretical possibility of non-capitalist price formation, they relied heavily on central planning institutions and offered limited scope for democratic participation in economic decision-making. The LangeLerner models essentially proposed technocratic solutions to the calculation problem, rather than addressing broader questions of economic democracy and worker control (Lavoie, 1985).

Contemporary market socialism has evolved significantly from these interwar models, incorporating insights from multiple sources: the failure of Soviet-type economies, which showed the practical limitations of central planning; advances in democratic theory that emphasize participation and autonomy; ecological economics that highlight the environmental costs of growth-oriented systems; and feminist economics that reveal the gendered nature of economic institutions (Kornai, 1992).

This theoretical evolution reflects both empirical evidence on the limitations of centralized planning and normative developments in socialist theory. The collapse of Soviet socialism provided decisive evidence that centralized economic planning could not ensure either efficiency or democracy, leading market socialists to develop more decentralized and participatory models (Nove, 1983).

The influence of the New Left and social movements of the 1960s also shaped contemporary market socialism by emphasizing participatory democracy, worker control, and the critique of bureaucratic authority. Thinkers like Carole Pateman and C.B. Macpherson argued that economic democracy was essential for meaningful political democracy, providing theoretical foundations for workplace democracy and participatory economic institutions (Pateman, 1970; Macpherson, 1977).

Environmental concerns have become increasingly central to market socialist theory as ecological limits become more apparent. Market socialists argue that democratic ownership and planning could redirect economic activity toward ecological sustainability, whereas capitalist market systems systematically prioritize short-term profits over long-term environmental stability (Burkett, 1999).

2.3.2 *Contemporary Theoretical Models: Diversity in Democratic Property*

Contemporary market socialism encompasses diverse theoretical models that differ in their approaches to property structures, market regulation, investment coordination, and democratic governance. These models share common commitments to eliminating capitalist exploitation while preserving market efficiency, but they differ significantly in their institutional prescriptions and theoretical foundations.

The influential analytical Marxist approach of John Roemer proposes models based on the egalitarian ownership of capital assets through social dividends, while retaining competitive markets for goods and labor (Roemer, 1994b). His "coupon socialism" envisions a system where citizens receive equal shares of social wealth in the form of non-transferable coupons that grant dividends from public firms. This model seeks to eliminate the concentration of wealth while preserving efficiency incentives by allowing firms to compete in input and output markets.

Roemer's approach uses rigorous microeconomic modeling to demonstrate that market socialist systems can achieve efficiency and equality under certain conditions. His models assume that public ownership of productive assets, combined with competitive markets for goods and services, will eliminate capitalist exploitation while maintaining the informational advantages of market prices. The non-transferable nature of the ownership coupons prevents the reconcentration of wealth that has historically undermined egalitarian initiatives (Roemer, 1994a).

However, critics argue that Roemer's model maintains too much separation between ownership and control, potentially reproducing many of the problems associated with contemporary shareholder capitalism. By treating citizens as passive dividend recipients rather than active participants in economic governance, coupon socialism may fail to achieve the democratic transformation of economic life that many socialists consider essential (Schweickart, 2011a).

David Schweickart's "Economic Democracy" model proposes a more participatory approach based on worker-managed firms that compete in a regulated market, with investment decisions made democratically at the local and regional levels (Schweickart, 2011a). This system would eliminate both the private ownership of productive assets and centralized state control, creating instead networks of worker cooperatives that would compete in markets while being accountable to their members.

In Economic Democracy, investment funds would be generated through taxes on productive assets and distributed to regions based on population, with local investment banks making lending decisions through democratic processes. This system would preserve market incentives for efficiency while ensuring that investment decisions serve community needs rather than maximizing returns for private capital. Worker-managed firms would compete in markets for goods and services but would distribute surpluses democratically rather than according to capital ownership (Schweickart, 2002).

Schweickart's model addresses several limitations of earlier proposals by emphasizing workplace democracy, community control over investment, and ecological sustainability. The democratic governance of firms and investment institutions would allow workers and communities to pursue goals beyond profit maximization, including environmental protection, work-life balance, and social solidarity.

Participatory economics (Parecon), developed by Michael Albert and Robin Hahnel, represents a more radical departure from market mechanisms while maintaining a commitment to decentralized coordination (Albert, 2003). Parecon proposes to replace both markets and central planning with participatory planning processes in which workers' and consumers' councils negotiate directly over production and consumption decisions.

The Parecon model emphasizes balanced job complexes that combine mental and manual labor to eliminate class divisions between mental and physical workers. Remuneration would be based on effort and sacrifice rather than output or bargaining power, while consumption decisions would be made through democratic councils rather than individual market choices. Critics argue that Parecon's planning procedures may be informationally demanding and politically cumbersome, while pro-ponents argue that digital technologies make such coordination increasingly feasible (Hahnel, 2005).

More recent theoretical developments have incorporated insights from commons research, ecological economics, and digital technology. Elinor Ostrom's work on common-pool resources has influenced market socialists interested in the democratic governance of shared assets, while platform cooperativism offers models of democratic ownership of digital infrastructures (Ostrom, 1990; Scholz, 2016).

Christian Fuchs and other "digital socialism" theorists advocate for democratically controlled digital platforms that could serve as foundations for post-capitalist economic coordination (Fuchs, 2014). These proposals envision social media platforms, search engines, and e-commerce sites owned by the public and governed by users rather than shareholders, eliminating surveillance capitalism while preserving the coordination benefits of digital networks.

The commons-based approach, influenced by Yochai Benkler and others, emphasizes peer production, open-source development, and creative commons licenses as alternatives to both private and state ownership (Benkler, 2006). This approach suggests that digital technologies enable new forms of non-market coordination that could gradually displace capitalist property relations.

Post-growth market socialism represents another significant theoretical development, incorporating ecological limits and degrowth economics into market socialist models. Theorists like John Bellamy Foster and Paul Burkett argue that democratic ownership is necessary for the transition to ecologically sustainable economic systems, as capitalist markets systematically prioritize growth over long-term ecological stability (Foster, 2009; Burkett, 1999).

2.3.3 *Institutional Design and Governance Mechanisms*

Contemporary market socialist theory devotes considerable attention to the institutional design challenges involved in creating democratic economic institutions that can function effectively in market environments. These design challenges include: creating governance structures that balance efficiency and democracy; developing incentive systems that motivate performance without reproducing class divisions; establishing coordination mechanisms that preserve market benefits while allowing for democratic planning; and designing regulatory frameworks that prevent the emergence of new forms of inequality and exploitation.

The governance of worker cooperatives raises complex questions about the relationship between democratic participation and operational efficiency. Research on existing cooperatives reveals tensions between member participation and managerial expertise, particularly in large organizations where direct democracy becomes cumbersome (Cornforth et al., 1995).

Market socialist theorists have proposed diverse solutions, including representative democracy with strong accountability mechanisms, rotation of leadership positions, and hybrid structures that combine democratic oversight with professional management.

The governance structure of the Mondragón Cooperative Corporation has been particularly influential in market socialist theory, demonstrating how large-scale cooperative networks can combine democratic ownership with market competition. Mondragón's system of elected management councils, educational institutions, and mutual support mechanisms offers a model for scaling cooperative principles beyond individual firms (Whyte & Whyte, 1991).

Investment coordination represents another crucial design challenge for market socialist systems. Unlike capitalist systems, where investment decisions are made by private owners seeking maximum returns, market socialism requires institutional mechanisms capable of channeling investment toward socially optimal projects while maintaining efficiency incentives. Diverse proposals have been developed, including democratic investment banks, participatory budgeting for public investment, and market-based mechanisms for directing social investment funds.

Schweickart's Economic Democracy model proposes regional investment banks that would be democratically controlled and tasked with allocating capital based on both economic and social criteria. These institutions would be funded through taxes on productive assets and would make lending decisions through democratic processes involving community representatives, technical experts, and affected workers (Schweickart, 2011a).

Regulatory frameworks for market socialist systems must address the tendency of market competition to generate inequality and for successful firms to accumulate advantages that could undermine democratic ownership. Various mechanisms have been proposed to address these challenges, including: limits on firm size to prevent the emergence of dominant firms; requirements for profit-sharing or worker ownership in all firms; progressive taxation of business income; and public provision of key infrastructure and services.

The relationship between market socialist firms and broader democratic institutions also requires careful institutional design. Market socialist theorists generally argue that workplace democracy must be complemented by broader forms of economic democracy, including community control over land use, democratic planning of infrastructure development, and citizen participation in macroeconomic policymaking.

2.3.4 Practical Examples and Contemporary Applications

Real-world examples of market socialist institutions, even while operating within predominantly capitalist systems, offer valuable insights into the practical challenges and possibilities of democratic economic organization. These examples include worker cooperatives, public banking systems, sovereign wealth funds, community land trusts, and various forms of social enterprise that combine market mechanisms with democratic ownership and social goals.

Worker cooperatives represent the most direct application of market socialist principles in contemporary economies. The global cooperative sector includes over one billion members and generates significant economic activity across diverse industries, from agriculture and retail to manufacturing and financial services (International Co-operative Alliance, 2018). Successful cooperatives demonstrate that democratic ownership can be compatible with market competition and economic efficiency.

The Mondragón Cooperative Corporation in the Basque Country represents one of the most developed examples of market socialist organization, combining worker ownership, democratic governance, and market competition through a network of over 260 firms (Whyte & Whyte, 1991). Founded in 1956 by Father José María Arizmendiarrieta, Mondragón has grown into the fourth-largest corporate group in Spain, with annual revenues exceeding €12 billion and over 80,000 worker-owners employed.

Mondragón's institutional structure includes several key elements that market socialist theorists have identified as crucial for democratic economic organization: democratic governance through elected councils and general assemblies; profitsharing based on labor contribution rather than capital ownership; limits on the wage ratios between the highest and lowest-paid workers; mutual support through internal banking and insurance systems; and investment in education and training through cooperative educational institutions.

The corporation's Caja Laboral (Workers' Bank) provides financial services to member cooperatives while also offering support for the development of new cooperatives. This internal banking system allows for democratic control over investment decisions and ensures that capital serves cooperative goals rather than pure profit maximization. The bank's business development services have been crucial for incubating new cooperatives and supporting existing ones during economic downturns. Mondragón's educational institutions, including a cooperative university and technical schools, show how democratic firms can invest in human development and technological innovation. The integration of education, research, and production within the cooperative network creates synergies that benefit both individual firms and the broader community.

However, Mondragón has also faced challenges that illustrate potential problems of market socialist organization. The corporation's expansion into international markets has led to the hiring of non-member workers in subsidiaries, creating tensions with cooperative principles. The 2008 financial crisis forced several Mondragón firms into bankruptcy, revealing vulnerabilities in the mutual support system. Some critics argue that Mondragón's success is partly dependent on the favorable cultural and political environment of the Basque Country, raising questions about the replicability of the model in other contexts (Kasmir, 1996).

Public banking institutions demonstrate how democratic control over finance can serve broader social goals while operating within market systems. The Bank of North Dakota, established in 1919, is the only state-owned bank in the United States and has played a crucial role in supporting local economic development, particularly in the agricultural and energy sectors (Brown, 2013). The bank's profits support state education and infrastructure rather than private shareholders, while its lending policies prioritize local development over maximum returns.

Similarly, the Kerala State Industrial Development Corporation in India shows how public financial institutions can support democratic development goals within market frameworks. KSIDC has funded cooperative enterprises, environmental projects, and social infrastructure while maintaining profitable operations (Isaac & Franke, 2005).

Sovereign wealth funds represent another form of market socialist institution that socializes the returns from natural resources or other public assets. Norway's Government Pension Fund Global, with assets exceeding $1.4 trillion, demonstrates how resource rents can be democratically managed and used to support social goals rather than private accumulation (Clark & Monk, 2008). The fund's ethical guidelines exclude investments in companies engaged in the production of weapons, tobacco, and environmental destruction, illustrating how democratic ownership can pursue values beyond profit maximization.

Alaska's Permanent Fund Dividend offers an example of how resource rents can be distributed directly to citizens, approximating Roemer's social dividend model. Since 1982, all Alaskan residents have received annual dividends from oil revenues, providing a form of basic income that has reduced poverty and supported the local economy. The program demonstrates the feasibility of socializing resource rents while maintaining market mechanisms for other economic activities (Widerquist & Howard, 2013).

Community land trusts (CLTs) represent another significant application of market socialist principles to land and housing markets. CLTs remove land from speculation through community ownership, allowing individuals to own buildings and improvements. This model preserves affordability while allowing market mechanisms to operate for housing improvements and maintenance (Davis, 2010).

The Burlington Community Land Trust in Vermont, established in 1984, has created permanently affordable housing while building community wealth and preventing displacement. The CLT model has been adopted in numerous cities as a tool for addressing housing affordability crises while maintaining democratic community control over land use decisions.

Platform cooperatives represent a contemporary application of market socialist principles to the digital economy. Examples include Stocksy United, a stock photography cooperative owned by its member photographers; Fairmondo, a cooperative alternative to Amazon; and CoopCycle, a cooperative delivery network (Scholz, 2016). These ventures demonstrate how cooperative principles can be applied to digital platforms while competing in online markets.

However, platform cooperatives face significant challenges in competing with venture capital-funded platforms, which can sustain losses while building market dominance. The network effects and winner-take-all dynamics of digital markets create barriers for cooperative alternatives that may require supportive public policies or alternative funding mechanisms to succeed.

Municipal broadband networks offer examples of how public ownership can be combined with market competition in technological sectors. Cities like Chattanooga, Tennessee, and municipal utilities across the United States have developed publicly owned broadband networks that compete with private providers while serving public goals like digital inclusion and economic development (Mitchell, 2016).

2.3.5 Challenges and Critiques: Theoretical and Practical Limitations

Market socialism faces significant theoretical and practical challenges that, according to its critics, could limit its viability as an alternative to capitalism. These challenges include: the persistence of market inequalities even under democratic ownership; the potential for bureaucratic ossification in democratic institutions; the difficulty of scaling cooperative principles to large and complex organizations; and the problem of maintaining democratic governance in competitive market environments.

The iron law of oligarchy, developed by Roberto Michels and applied to cooperatives by various scholars, suggests that democratic organizations tend to become oligarchic over time as complexity increases and expertise becomes concentrated (Michels, 1915). Critics argue that market socialist firms could reproduce class divisions between managers and workers, even under formally democratic ownership. Research on worker cooperatives reveals mixed evidence regarding democratic participation. While many cooperatives maintain strong member engagement and democratic governance, others show low rates of participation and effective control by small groups of active members or professional managers (Rothschild & Whitt, 2009). The challenge of maintaining meaningful democracy in large organizations remains unresolved in market socialist theory.

Market competition itself can generate pressures that undermine democratic governance and social goals. Firms facing competitive pressure may prioritize efficiency over democracy, leading to the erosion of participatory institutions. The need to compete with capitalist firms may force market socialist firms to adopt similar practices regarding labor discipline, technological development, and cost cutting.

The problem of capital accumulation represents another challenge for market socialist systems. Successful firms may accumulate surpluses that could be reinvested to expand operations, potentially creating advantages that undermine equality among firms. Various mechanisms have been proposed to address this challenge, including progressive taxation, limits on firm size, and requirements for surplus sharing, but the effectiveness of these measures remains debated.

Investment coordination poses ongoing theoretical and practical challenges for market socialist systems. While market prices provide information about current supply and demand conditions, they may not adequately signal future investment needs or social priorities. Democratic investment institutions must balance technical expertise with democratic participation, creating potential tensions between efficiency and democracy.

The problem of the "free-rider" can affect democratic governance in market socialist firms. If the benefits of participating in governance are shared among all members while the costs are borne by active participants, rational individuals might choose to minimize their involvement while free-riding on the efforts of others. This dynamic could undermine the democratic character of market socialist institutions over time.

Environmental critics argue that market socialism may not adequately address ecological limits if it maintains competitive pressures for growth and efficiency. While democratic ownership could enable firms to pursue environmental goals, market competition might still generate incentives for resource consumption and waste production that conflict with ecological sustainability (Kovel, 2007).

2.3.6 Contemporary Relevance and Future Prospects

The contemporary relevance of market socialism has been reinforced by several developments: the growing level of inequality under neoliberal capitalism; the demonstrated failures of centralized planning; technological advances that facilitate democratic coordination; and increasing environmental pressures that require alternatives to growth-oriented systems.

The platform economy has created new opportunities for market socialist organization through platform cooperatives and commons-based peer production. Digital technologies allow for new forms of democratic participation and coordination that could address some of the traditional challenges of scale and complexity in market socialist institutions (Bauwens, 2005).

The growth of the gig economy has generated new interest in cooperative alternatives to platform capitalism. Worker cooperatives and platform cooperatives offer models for organizing freelance and independent workers, providing greater economic security and democratic control than traditional employment or independent contracting.

Climate change has renewed interest in market socialist approaches to environmental problems. Democratic ownership and planning could enable the rapid economic transformation required to address climate change, while market mechanisms could provide efficiency incentives for resource use and technological innovation within ecological limits.

The COVID-19 pandemic has demonstrated both the importance of public institutions and the limitations of market-oriented healthcare and social protection systems. This experience has generated new interest in the democratic public ownership of essential services and infrastructure.

Contemporary market socialist proposals increasingly emphasize gradual transformation rather than revolutionary change. Strategies for expanding market socialist institutions include: supporting cooperative development through public policies; creating public banks and investment funds; developing community ownership of renewable energy systems; and promoting employee stock ownership plans and worker buyouts of existing firms.

The relationship between market socialism and broader social movements remains an important area of development. Environmental, labor, and community development movements increasingly recognize the connections between economic democracy and their specific goals, creating potential coalitions for advancing market socialist policies and institutions.

However, market socialism continues to face challenges from both neoliberal capitalism and authoritarian socialism. The global dominance of capitalist markets creates competitive pressures that can undermine cooperative enterprises, while authoritarian tendencies in some socialist movements may discourage democratic economic experimentation.

The future of market socialism may depend on its ability to address contemporary challenges like digitalization, the environmental crisis, and economic inequality, while learning from historical experiences and ongoing experiments in democratic economic organization.

2.4 Points of Convergence with Situationist Critique

Although the Situationist International (SI) rejected institutional mediation as inherently complicit in the reproduction of the spectacle, certain reformist proposals associated with social democracy and market socialism can be interpreted as partial realizations of Situationist goals, particularly when they challenge the commodification of everyday life and create conditions for autonomous activity (Vaneigem, 1967). This apparent contradiction between the SI's anti-institutional stance and the potential for institutional reforms to advance Situationist goals reflects deeper tensions within radical theory about the relationship between revolutionary transformation and incremental change.

The SI's rejection of reformism was based on its analysis of how spectacular society recuperates potentially subversive forces, transforming them into mechanisms for reproducing the system rather than genuine liberation. However, contemporary analysis suggests that certain reforms can generate contradictions within spectacular capitalism that open up space for more radical transformations, particularly when they address fundamental aspects of commodification and alienation (Holloway, 2002).

Four areas appear especially promising for this convergence: universal basic income as a mechanism for decommodifying survival; the reduction of working time as a strategy of temporal liberation; participatory urbanism as a means of spatial liberation; and the democratic management of resources as a path toward economic democracy. Each of these areas addresses core concerns of Situationist theory while remaining potentially compatible with reformist political strategies.

The analysis of these convergences requires attention to both their liberating potential and their risks of recuperation. As the SI demonstrated, spectacular society has a remarkable capacity to absorb and neutralize potentially subversive forces, transforming radical critiques into marketing strategies and revolutionary demands into policy proposals that ultimately serve the maintenance of the system rather than its transformation.

2.4.1 Universal Basic Income and Decommodification: Beyond Wage Slavery

Universal Basic Income (UBI), defined as unconditional cash transfers to all citizens regardless of their work status, merit, or need, has gained significant attention across the political spectrum as a response to technological unemployment, labor precarity, and the inadequacies of the welfare state (Van Parijs & Vanderborght, 2017). The concept's appeal spans from Silicon Valley entrepreneurs concerned with technological displacement to social democrats seeking to strengthen welfare universalism and market socialists proposing new forms of wealth redistribution.

From a social democratic perspective, UBI represents a logical extension of welfare universalism that addresses the limitations of contributory and means-tested benefit systems. Guy Standing argues that UBI could provide security in increasingly precarious labor markets while simplifying welfare administration and reducing bureaucratic control over beneficiaries' lives (Standing, 2017). This approach views UBI as compatible with existing welfare states, potentially replacing some programs while strengthening the social safety net.

Social democratic proponents emphasize UBI's potential to address technological unemployment and the growth of precarious labor relations that traditional unemployment insurance systems cannot adequately cover. The rise of platform work, zero-hour contracts, and the gig economy generates new forms of insecurity that existing welfare systems struggle to address (Standing, 2011).

From a market socialist perspective, UBI can be conceptualized as a mechanism for socializing the returns to capital and redistributing wealth while maintaining market efficiency and incentives for productive activity (Roemer, 1996). This approach emphasizes funding UBI through progressive taxation, land value capture, or the socialization of natural resource rents, rather than labor taxes that could undermine work incentives.

The Alaska Permanent Fund Dividend, established in 1982 and funded by oil revenues, stands as the longest-running example of a quasi-UBI system, demonstrating both the political feasibility and economic effects of universal cash transfers (Goldsmith, 2010). The program has provided annual payments of $1000 to $2072 per person, creating a modest but significant income floor, and enjoys broad popular support across political divides.

Research on the Alaska dividend suggests positive effects on poverty reduction, especially for children, with no significant negative impacts on work incentives. The program has also demonstrated remarkable political durability, surviving attempts at reduction or elimination by both Republican and Democratic governors (Widerquist & Howard, 2013).

In Situationist terms, UBI resonates powerfully with the core critiques of wage labor and the demands for liberation from the compulsion to work that were central to Debord and Vaneigem's analyses of the spectacular society. By unlinking subsistence from employment, UBI creates the material conditions to refuse meaningless jobs and pursue autonomous activities outside the sphere of commodification (Weeks, 2011).

The Situationist critique of work was not limited to reducing working hours or improving conditions, but to challenging the fundamental organization of social life around commodity production and wage labor. Debord argued that the spectacular society colonizes all aspects of human activity, transforming creative potential into abstract labor power and reducing human relationships to market transactions (Debord, 1967).

UBI's potential to support Situationist goals lies in its capacity to create what Erik Olin Wright calls "real freedom"—the material capacity to pursue chosen activities rather than activities dictated by the need for survival (Wright, 2006). This freedom could allow people to engage in creative activities, social experimentation, care work, political participation, and other forms of meaningful activity that resist commodification.

André Gorz, whose later work linked Situationist insights with contemporary post-work debates, argued that a guaranteed income could allow for an "exit from the society of work," making it possible for individuals to invest time and energy in creativity, care, and social bonds rather than wage labor (Gorz, 1989). His analysis emphasized that liberation from the compulsion to work was necessary to develop human capacities that capitalist production systematically represses.

Contemporary post-work theorists like Kathi Weeks have developed these ideas, arguing that UBI could support what she calls "life beyond work"—forms of social organization that prioritize human flourishing over economic productivity (Weeks, 2011). This perspective emphasizes UBI's potential to challenge the work ethic that justifies inequality and legitimizes capitalist exploitation.

Recent empirical evidence from UBI experiments provides some support for these theoretical arguments. The Finnish Basic Income Experiment (2017–2018) found that UBI recipients experienced reduced stress, improved mental health, and greater trust in social institutions compared to control groups receiving traditional unemployment benefits (Kangas et al., 2019). Recipients also engaged in more creative activities, education, and care work, suggesting that income security can enable the pursuit of intrinsically valuable activities.

The Stockton Economic Empowerment Demonstration (SEED) in California found that UBI recipients spent the vast majority of their income on basic needs like food, housing, and transportation, contradicting stereotypes about the spending of transfers on drugs or alcohol (West et al., 2021). They also reported reduced anxiety and a greater ability to seek employment, suggesting that income security can enhance, rather than undermine, economic participation.

The GiveDirectly experiment in Kenya, which provides long-term cash transfers to rural villages, has shown significant positive effects on economic development, education, and health outcomes while allowing recipients to invest in small businesses, education, and community infrastructure (Haushofer & Shapiro, 2016).

However, the Situationist potential of UBI faces significant challenges and risks of recuperation. Critics from multiple political perspectives have raised concerns about its compatibility with capitalist accumulation and its potential to serve neoliberal rather than emancipatory goals.

Left-wing critics argue that UBI could function as a "Trojan horse" for neoliberal welfare retrenchment, providing minimal support while justifying the elimination of more comprehensive social programs like universal healthcare, public education, and social housing (Zamora, 2017). This "libertarian" version of UBI, supported by figures like Charles Murray and Milton Friedman, would replace existing programs with cash transfers while reducing overall social spending.

The risk of UBI functioning as a subsidy for low-wage employers represents another significant concern. If UBI allows workers to accept lower wages by supplementing their income, it could subsidize exploitative labor relations rather than challenge them, reproducing the commodification of labor that the Situationists rejected.

Daniel Zamora and other critics argue that UBI reflects an acceptance of permanent mass unemployment and social exclusion rather than a challenge to the economic system that produces these conditions (Zamora, 2017). From this perspective, UBI represents an accommodation to the capitalist crisis rather than a strategy for transcending capitalism.

UBI's relationship with commodification is particularly complex. While it could reduce dependence on wage labor, it maintains the money form and market relations that the Situationists viewed as inherently alienating. Recipients remain consumers in market systems, potentially reproducing spectacular consumption patterns rather than challenging them.

The political economy of UBI implementation also raises important questions about its emancipatory potential. Programs require significant public revenue, typically generated through taxation or resource extraction. The political coalitions required to implement it may require compromises that limit its transformative potential or embed it in existing power structures.

The support of tech companies for UBI partially reflects their interest in maintaining consumer demand as automation reduces employment opportunities. This instrumental support suggests that UBI could serve capital accumulation rather than challenge it, by ensuring the continued consumption of goods produced by increasingly automated systems.

The Situationist potential of UBI thus depends largely on its design, funding mechanism, political context, and relationship to broader strategies of social transformation. A transformative UBI should be: generous enough to offer genuine alternatives to wage labor; funded through progressive mechanisms that redistribute wealth and power rather than just income; integrated into broader strategies for democratizing economic institutions and challenging commodity relations; and designed to support collective organization and social experimentation rather than individualized consumption.

Recent proposals for "participatory income" or "social inheritance" attempt to address some of these concerns by linking economic support to contributions to social reproduction, care work, or community development rather than providing unconditional transfers (Atkinson, 2015). These approaches seek to recognize and support socially valuable activities that markets do not reward, while preventing UBI from subsidizing social withdrawal.

2.4.2 Reduction of Working Time and Temporal Liberation: Reclaiming Life from Accumulation

The struggle for shorter working hours has been central to labor movements since the Industrial Revolution, representing both immediate demands for better working conditions and broader visions of human liberation from capitalist temporal discipline (Cross, 1988). Contemporary proposals for four-day workweeks, six-hour days, or more radical reductions in standard working time draw on this historical tradition while addressing new concerns about ecological sustainability, technological automation, and work-life balance in post-industrial societies.

The historical development of working time struggles reveals their connection to broader questions of social organization and human freedom. The late 19thcentury movement for the eight-hour day combined immediate demands for better working conditions with utopian visions of a balanced social life organized into eight hours of work, eight hours of rest, and eight hours of leisure (Roediger & Foner, 1986). This formula represented not just a quantitative reduction in working time but a qualitative transformation of the allocation of social time that would enable working-class cultural development and political participation.

John Maynard Keynes's famous prediction that technological progress would allow for a fifteen-hour workweek by the early twenty-first century reflected similar assumptions about the relationship between productivity growth and human liberation (Keynes, 1930). Keynes envisioned a future in which material abundance would free humanity from economic necessity, allowing it to focus on art, culture, and personal development beyond mere survival.

The failure of these predictions has generated important theoretical and empirical research on the persistence of long working hours despite dramatic increases in productivity. Juliet Schor's influential analysis demonstrates that working hours in the United States increased in the second half of the twentieth century, despite technological advances that could have allowed for significant reductions (Schor, 1991).

Contemporary proposals for working time reduction arise from multiple motivations: addressing technological unemployment by redistributing available work; improving work-life balance and reducing stress-related health problems; advancing gender equality by allowing for a more equitable distribution of care work; reducing environmental impact by limiting production and consumption; and creating space for non-market activities that contribute to human well-being (Schor, 2005).

Recent experiments with working time reduction in various countries provide empirical evidence on its effects on productivity, well-being, and social outcomes. The Icelandic trials of four-day workweeks between 2015 and 2019, which involved over 2500 workers in public and private sectors, demonstrated that reducing hours could maintain productivity while significantly improving worker well-being and work-life balance (Haraldsson & Kellam, 2021).

The Icelandic experiments found that workers reported lower stress, better health, improved work-life balance, and more time for family, friends, and personal interests. Productivity remained stable or improved in most workplaces as organizations adapted by eliminating unnecessary meetings, reducing interruptions, and focusing on essential tasks. The success of these trials led to permanent reductions in working time for the vast majority of Iceland's labor force.

Similar experiments in Belgium, Scotland, and Spain have yielded comparable results, suggesting that working time reduction can improve individual and social outcomes without sacrificing economic performance. Microsoft Japan's 2019 four-day workweek trial resulted in a 40% increase in productivity while maintaining employee satisfaction and reducing energy consumption.

From a Situationist perspective, working time reduction addresses fundamental critiques how capitalist temporal discipline colonizes human experience and constrains the possibilities for authentic activity. The SI's analysis emphasized that the spectacular society commodifies time itself, organizing social life around the rhythms of production and consumption rather than human needs and desires (Debord, 1967).

Debord's critique of "spectacular time" analyzes how media, advertising, and consumer culture create artificial temporal rhythms that disconnect individuals from natural and social cycles. The spectacle colonizes leisure time as much as work time, transforming rest and recreation into opportunities for commodity consumption and passive spectatorship rather than active creation and genuine encounter.

Vaneigem's analysis of everyday life emphasized how wage labor and commodity relations constrain temporal experience, reducing life to mechanical repetition and preventing the development of creative capacity (Vaneigem, 1967). Liberation of time from capitalist control was essential to enabling what Vaneigem termed "the revolution of everyday life"—the transformation of daily experience from alienated survival to authentic living.

For the SI, working time reduction aligned with broader demands for the liberation of everyday life from the imperatives of accumulation and bureaucratic control. Reduced working hours, combined with access to resources and opportunities for participatory activity, could open up possibilities for play, the *dérive*, collective experimentation, and the construction of situations that challenge spectacular passivity.

However, the Situationist analysis also emphasized that working time reduction alone would not automatically produce liberating outcomes. Without complementary cultural and institutional changes, reduced hours could simply expand commodified consumption, individualized leisure, or what Debord termed "pseudoactivity"—forms of apparent participation that actually reinforce spectacular relations.

The SI's practice of the *dérive* provides insights into how liberated time could be used for non-alienated activity. The *dérive* involved experimental wandering through urban environments, abandoning functional purpose and allowing oneself to be guided by encounters and attractions that revealed new spatial and social possibilities (Debord, 1956). This practice required both free time and the cultural capacity to use it creatively and non-consumptively.

Contemporary research on working time reduction suggests that its effects depend significantly on how liberated time is used and the broader social context in which the reduction occurs. Studies indicate that shorter workweeks can allow for greater participation in care work, education, community activities, and political engagement, but they could also simply expand passive consumption such as television, shopping, or other activities (Golden, 2012b).

The gender dimensions of working time reduction deserve particular attention, given the SI's relative neglect of feminist concerns. Research indicates that working time reduction can advance gender equality by allowing for a more equitable distribution of care work, but only if it is accompanied by cultural changes in gender role expectations and institutional support for caring activities (Gornick & Meyers, 2003).

The experience of Nordic countries with parental leave policies demonstrates how working time reduction can be designed to promote gender equality. Norway's "father's quota" system, which reserves part of the parental leave specifically for fathers, has increased male participation in childcare and reduced career penalties for women (Brandth & Kvande, 2012).

Ecological arguments for working time reduction have gained relevance as environmental crises intensify. Shorter workweeks can reduce environmental impact through multiple mechanisms: lower commuting and workplace energy consumption; decreased production and consumption pressures; greater time for sustainable practices like home food production and repair; and a reduction in stress-driven consumption (Knight, 2012).

However, the relationship between working time reduction and environmental sustainability is complex and depends on broader economic and cultural patterns. Reduced hours could enable travel, leisure consumption, or other environmentally damaging activities if not accompanied by cultural shifts toward sustainable lifestyles (Pullinger, 2014).

The post-growth economics literature has increasingly emphasized working time reduction as essential for the transition to steady-state economies that operate within planetary boundaries. Tim Jackson argues that shorter workweeks are necessary to maintain employment levels while reducing the economic throughput to sustainable levels (Jackson, 2017).

Automation and artificial intelligence provide additional arguments for working time reduction by potentially displacing human labor in large sectors of the economy. Rather than accepting technological unemployment, working time reduction could allow for a more equitable distribution of remaining human work while providing time for activities that resist automation—care, creativity, community building, and environmental restoration (Srnicek & Williams, 2017).

The political economy of working time reduction raises important questions about its implementation in capitalist systems. Employers may resist shorter workweeks due to fixed costs of employment, coordination challenges, and competitive pressures. Labor movements face strategic questions about whether to prioritize hour reduction over wage increases or other demands.

The experience of France with the 35-hour workweek, implemented in 2000, illustrates both possibilities and limitations of legislative approaches to working time reduction. The policy succeeded in generating employment and improving work-life balance but faced resistance from employers and was partially rolled back by subsequent governments under pressure from business interests (Cette et al., 2013b).

Collective bargaining approaches to working time reduction may be more sustainable than legislative mandates, as they can be adapted to specific industries and workplaces while strengthening worker organization. The German trade union movement's campaigns for shorter hours in the 1980s and recent union initiatives in various countries suggest a renewed interest in this approach (Hinrichs et al., 1991). The Situationist potential of working time reduction ultimately depends on its integration with broader strategies of cultural and institutional transformation. Liberated time must be accompanied by: access to resources and opportunities for creative activity; cultural alternatives to consumerist leisure; spaces and institutions that support collective experimentation; and political movements that challenge the broader structures of capitalist accumulation that constrain temporal liberation.

2.4.3 *Participatory Urbanism and Spatial Liberation: Cities as Sites of Collective Creation*

2.4.3.1 *Participatory Urbanism*

Note that participatory urbanism is treated here less as an established alternative than as an emergent field whose emancipatory potential remains uneven and highly contingent. From a Situationist perspective, urban space has long been a central terrain of struggle over everyday life, mobility, and the organization of time.

Urban space held a central position in Situationist critique and experimental practice, reflecting their understanding that spatial organization reflects and reproduces broader social relations of domination and liberation. The SI opposed modernist urban planning that reduced cities to functional zones of work, residence, and consumption, viewing this as expressing and reinforcing the spectacular separation of life into discrete and alienated spheres (Sadler, 1998).

The Situationist critique of urban planning was based on Henri Lefebvre's analysis of the "production of space" and his argument that spatial organization serves ideological functions by naturalizing social relations and limiting the possibilities for alternative forms of social organization (Lefebvre, 1991b). Lefebvre's influence on the SI was particularly evident in their analysis of how capitalist urbanization transforms cities from sites of encounter and possibility into mechanisms of social control and commodity circulation.

The SI's practices of the *dérive* and their theoretical proposals for "unitarian urbanism" envisioned cities as laboratories for collective creativity and experimentation, not just as functional spaces for economic activity (Kotanyi & Vaneigem, 1961). Unitarian urbanism would integrate architecture, urban planning, and social organization to create environments conducive to authentic experience and revolutionary transformation.

Contemporary movements for participatory urbanism reflect aspects of this Situationist vision, adapting it to current conditions of urban development, gentrification, and environmental crisis. These movements range from participatory budgeting initiatives, which give residents direct control over public investment decisions, to tactical urbanism interventions that temporarily transform public spaces to showcase alternative possibilities (Baiocchi, 2005; Russell, 2019).

The "right to the city" tradition, based on Lefebvre's work and extended by David Harvey, provides a theoretical framework for understanding participatory urbanism as a form of spatial politics that challenges capitalist control over urban development (Lefebvre, 1968; Harvey, 2008). Harvey argues that the right to the city does not just entail access to urban resources but collective power to reshape cities according to social needs rather than profit imperatives.

Participatory budgeting, pioneered in Porto Alegre, Brazil, in the late 1980s, represents one of the most developed forms of participatory urbanism, giving residents direct decision-making power over portions of the municipal budget through neighborhood assemblies and city-level councils (Baiocchi, 2005). The Porto Alegre model has been adopted in thousands of cities globally, demonstrating the feasibility of democratic participation in urban governance.

Research on participatory budgeting indicates positive effects on the quality of public investment, citizen participation, and social inclusion, especially for marginalized communities that normally lack influence in conventional political processes. Studies show that participatory budgeting tends to redirect public investment toward poor neighborhoods and social infrastructure, rather than elite-oriented projects (Wampler, 2007).

Barcelona's recent experiments with participatory democracy, including neighborhood assemblies, citizen panels, and digital participation platforms, illustrate how participatory urbanism can be scaled to major metropolitan areas. The city's Decidim platform allows residents to propose, debate, and vote on policy initiatives while participating in neighborhood assemblies that have real decision-making power on local issues (Calleja-López et al., 2017).

Community land trusts (CLTs) represent another significant form of participatory urbanism that addresses housing affordability while maintaining democratic community control over land use. CLTs take land out of speculation by holding it in permanent community ownership, allowing individuals to own the buildings and improvements, thereby creating permanently affordable housing and enabling democratic governance of neighborhood development (Davis, 2010).

The Burlington Community Land Trust in Vermont has preserved housing affordability for over three decades while building community wealth and preventing displacement. Residents participate in democratic governance through community assemblies and elected boards that make decisions about land use, development priorities, and community programming.

Tactical urbanism interventions—temporary installations that showcase alternative uses of public space—provide examples of how Situationist practices could be adapted to contemporary urban conditions. These interventions range from pop-up parks and guerrilla gardens to temporary bike lanes and street art that challenges dominant uses of space (Moore & Wilson, 2018).

The transformation of Times Square and the High Line in New York, from trafficdominated spaces to pedestrian environments, demonstrates how tactical interventions can evolve into permanent changes in urban design. These projects show how temporary experiments can build support for broader transformations of urban space.

However, participatory urbanism faces significant structural limitations that constrain its transformative potential. Market pressures, real estate speculation, and regulatory frameworks often limit participatory possibilities, while gentrification can displace communities before they benefit from participatory improvements in their neighborhoods.

The cooptation of participatory urbanism by real estate interests and municipal authorities represents a significant concern. Participatory processes can be used to legitimize predetermined development decisions rather than enabling genuine democratic control, while improvements generated through participation can increase property values and contribute to the displacement of existing residents.

Barcelona's experience illustrates both the possibilities and limitations of participatory urbanism within capitalist urban development. While the city has implemented innovative participatory mechanisms, it continues to face pressures from tourism, real estate speculation, and European Union austerity policies that limit municipal autonomy (Russell, 2012).

From a Situationist perspective, the liberating potential of participatory urbanism lies in its ability to challenge the spectacular control over spatial experience and transform cities from commodified environments into sites of collective experimentation and creative encounter. The SI's vision of unitarian urbanism emphasized the integration of artistic practice, spatial design, and social organization to create environments that would facilitate the revolutionary transformation of everyday life. Contemporary participatory urbanism movements sometimes approximate this vision by creating spaces and processes that allow for collective creativity, democratic decision-making, and experimental approaches to urban life. Community gardens, cooperative housing projects, neighborhood assemblies, and cultural centers can function as "free spaces" that prefigure alternative forms of social organization.

The Situationist practice of *détournement* finds contemporary expression in tactical urbanism interventions that appropriate and transform existing urban infrastructure to showcase alternative possibilities. Street art, guerrilla gardening, and temporary installations that challenge dominant uses of public space can reveal hidden potentials in urban environments while building capacity for broader transformation.

However, the integration of participatory urbanism with broader strategies of social transformation remains a significant challenge. Many participatory initiatives remain limited to consultation rather than genuine co-production, while others become isolated experiments that do not challenge the broader structures of urban development and spatial inequality.

The commodification of participation represents a significant risk, as participatory processes can be coopted by development interests seeking to legitimize profitdriven projects through superficial community engagement. The challenge is to develop participatory practices that maintain their experimental and democratic character while advancing toward the broader transformation of urban development processes.

Climate change and the environmental crisis create new imperatives for participatory urbanism, as cities must rapidly transform to reduce carbon emissions and adapt to climate impacts. Participatory approaches to urban sustainability—including community-owned renewable energy systems, participatory environmental planning, and the democratic governance of urban commons—could integrate ecological and social transformation.

The COVID-19 pandemic has demonstrated both the importance of public space and the potential for rapid transformation of urban environments when social priorities shift. The temporary conversion of streets to pedestrian and cycling spaces, the expansion of outdoor dining, and the creation of new public spaces show how quickly cities can be reconfigured when there is political will.

Digital technologies create new possibilities for participatory urbanism through online platforms that allow for broader participation in planning processes, real-time feedback on urban policies, and the integration of citizen-generated data into urban governance. However, digital participation also raises concerns about the exclusion of residents without internet access and the potential for surveillance of participatory activities.

The Situationist potential of participatory urbanism ultimately depends on its ability to: challenge the private property relations that limit democratic control over urban development; create genuine alternatives to commodified urban space rather than simply humanizing existing development patterns; integrate spatial transformation with broader cultural and economic changes; and build collective capacity for ongoing experimentation and democratic governance, rather than one-off participation exercises.

2.4.4 *Democratic Resource Management and Economic Democracy: Socializing Strategic Assets*

Democratic control over strategic resources such as finance, energy, natural monopolies, and essential infrastructure represents a fourth domain where reformist proposals can converge with Situationist goals by challenging capitalist control over the material bases of everyday life. Market socialist theorists emphasize that social ownership of capital and democratic allocation of investment can prevent the concentration of wealth while orienting resources toward collective priorities rather than private profit maximization (Schweickart, 2011a).

The Situationist analysis identified capitalist control over production as central to the reproduction of the spectacle, arguing that private ownership of productive assets allows capital to dictate the terms of everyday life and limit the possibilities for authentic experience and collective experimentation (Debord, 1967). Democratic resource management breaks this control by subjecting investment decisions and resource allocation to democratic deliberation, rather than relying solely on market signals.

Contemporary examples of democratic resource management include public banking systems, community-owned energy grids, cooperative enterprises, sovereign wealth funds, and various forms of commons governance that demonstrate alternatives to the private ownership of strategic assets. These institutions show how democratic control can be combined with market mechanisms to achieve both efficiency and equity in resource allocation.

Public banking represents one of the most developed forms of democratic finance, demonstrating how communities can retain control over investment decisions while operating within market systems. The Bank of North Dakota, established in 1919 as the only state-owned bank in the United States, has played a crucial role in supporting local economic development, particularly in the agricultural and energy sectors (Brown, 2013).

The Bank of North Dakota operates as a commercial bank while serving public purposes: its profits support state education and infrastructure rather than private shareholders; its lending policies prioritize local development over maximum returns; and its investment decisions are subject to democratic oversight through elected officials and public accountability mechanisms. The bank's success in maintaining profitability while serving public goals demonstrates the viability of public ownership in financial services.

Germany's public savings banks (Sparkassen) and cooperative banks provide additional examples of democratically controlled financial institutions that operate successfully within market systems. These institutions, which control approximately 40% of German banking assets, are owned by local governments or member cooperatives rather than private shareholders, which allows them to prioritize community development and long-term stability over short-term profits (Ayadi et al., 2010).

Research indicates that regions with stronger public and cooperative banking sectors experienced less severe impacts during the 2008 financial crisis, suggesting that democratic ownership can provide greater stability and resilience than private ownership (Ferri et al., 2014). Additionally, public and cooperative banks tend to provide better access to credit for small businesses and lower-income communities that private banks often neglect.

The Kerala State Industrial Development Corporation (KSIDC) in India demonstrates how public financial institutions can support democratic development goals within market frameworks. KSIDC has funded cooperative enterprises, environmental projects, and social infrastructure while maintaining profitable operations and democratic governance through elected boards and community participation (Isaac & Franke, 2005).

Community-owned renewable energy systems represent another significant form of democratic resource management that combines environmental sustainability with economic democracy. The experience of Denmark in cooperative wind energy development demonstrates how democratic ownership can accelerate the adoption of renewable energy while building local wealth and capacity (Mendonça et al., 2009). Danish energy cooperatives, developed out of local initiatives in the 1970s and 1980s, allowed communities to own and operate wind turbines while selling electricity to the grid. This model created economic incentives for renewable energy development, ensuring that the benefits remained in local communities rather than flowing to distant shareholders.

The German energy transition (Energiewende) has relied heavily on community ownership and cooperative development of renewable energy, with over 50% of renewable energy capacity held by individuals, farmers, and energy cooperatives rather than large corporations (Yildiz et al., 2015). This model of distributed ownership has accelerated the adoption of renewable energy while democratizing the governance of the energy system.

Sovereign wealth funds represent large-scale examples of resource socialization that show possibilities for democratizing the rents derived from natural resources and other public assets. Norway's Government Pension Fund Global, with assets exceeding $1.4 trillion from oil revenues, demonstrates how resource rents can be democratically managed and used to support social goals rather than private accumulation (Clark & Monk, 2008).

The Norwegian fund operates under ethical guidelines established through democratic processes that exclude investments in companies engaged in the production of weapons, tobacco, and environmental destruction. The fund's governance includes parliamentary oversight, public reporting requirements, and citizen participation in the development of ethical policies, illustrating how democratic accountability can be maintained even in the management of large-scale investments.

The Alaska Permanent Fund Dividend offers a complementary example of how resource rents can be distributed directly to citizens, approximating the social dividend models proposed by market socialist theorists. Since 1982, all Alaskan residents have received annual dividends from oil revenues, providing a form of basic income that has reduced poverty and supported local economies while demonstrating the political viability of resource socialization (Widerquist & Howard, 2013).

Cooperative enterprises represent perhaps the most direct application of democratic resource management principles, demonstrating how worker ownership and democratic governance can operate within market systems while challenging capitalist property relations. The global cooperative sector includes over one billion members and generates significant economic activity in industries ranging from agriculture and retail to manufacturing and financial services (International Co-operative Alliance, 2018).

Research on cooperative firms indicates that they tend to be more resilient during economic downturns, provide more stable employment, and invest more in worker training and community development than comparable capitalist firms. Additionally, cooperatives tend to have more compressed wage ratios and more democratic workplace cultures, suggesting that democratic ownership can advance both economic democracy and social equity (Pencavel et al., 2012).

From a Situationist perspective, the liberating potential of democratic resource management lies in its ability to disrupt capital's control over the material conditions of everyday life, creating spaces for collective experimentation and autonomous activity. By reorienting investment from profit maximization toward social and ecological goals, democratic resource management could expand the spheres of autonomy and creativity while reducing dependence on consumer goods.

The SI's critique emphasized that capitalist control over production allows capital to determine not only the conditions of labor but the entire organization of social life: urban development, technological development, cultural production, and even the rhythm and content of daily experience (Vaneigem, 1967). Democratic control over strategic resources could challenge this comprehensive domination by subjecting investment decisions to collective deliberation and social priorities.

However, democratic resource management faces significant challenges and risks of recuperation that could limit its transformative potential. Market pressures can constrain the ability of democratic institutions to pursue social goals if these conflict with competitive imperatives. Bureaucratic tendencies within democratic institutions can reproduce hierarchical relations and technocratic decision-making that exclude meaningful participation.

The integration of democratic resource management institutions within broader capitalist systems raises questions about their ability to challenge, rather than simply humanize, capitalist accumulation. Public banks and cooperative firms can improve conditions for workers and communities while ultimately serving capital accumulation by providing infrastructure and services that private markets cannot profitably offer.

The environmental crisis provides additional arguments for democratizing resource management, as capitalist growth imperatives appear increasingly incompatible with planetary limits and ecological sustainability. Democratic control over energy systems, in particular, could enable rapid transitions to renewable energy while ensuring that the benefits are distributed equitably rather than concentrated among shareholders.

Climate change adaptation and mitigation require massive public investment and coordination that may be impossible to achieve through private markets alone. Democratic resource management institutions could provide mechanisms for mobilizing resources and coordinating the transformation while maintaining democratic accountability and social equity (Mazzucato, 2021).

The COVID-19 pandemic demonstrated both the importance of public investment and the capacity for rapid economic transformation when social priorities shift. Government responses included massive public investments in healthcare, income support, and economic stabilization, resembling wartime mobilization, while revealing possibilities for democratic economic coordination.

Digital technologies create new possibilities for democratic resource management through platforms that allow for broader participation in investment decisions, real-time monitoring of resource use, and integration of citizen input into resource allocation processes. Blockchain technologies could enable new forms of commons governance and cooperative ownership that scale democratic resource management beyond local communities.

However, digital technologies also create new forms of monopoly control and surveillance that require democratic responses. The concentration of digital platform ownership in a few corporations demonstrates the importance of extending democratic resource management to digital infrastructure and data commons (Srnicek, 2017).

The Situationist potential of democratic resource management ultimately depends on its integration with broader strategies of cultural and institutional transformation. Democratic control of resources must be accompanied by: cultural alternatives to consumerist lifestyles that reduce resource dependency; participatory institutions that enable meaningful democratic engagement rather than mere formal accountability; and political movements that challenge the broader structures of capitalist accumulation rather than simply redistributing its benefits.

2.4.5 Synthesis and Critical Evaluation: Possibilities and Limitations of Convergence

The analysis of the points of convergence between Situationist critique and reformist proposals reveals both significant possibilities and fundamental limitations for achieving revolutionary transformation through institutional reform. While universal basic income (UBI), working time reduction, participatory urbanism, and democratic resource management each address central concerns of Situationist theory, their ability to transcend, rather than merely ameliorate, spectacular capitalism depends critically on their design, implementation, and integration with broader transformative strategies.

The theoretical foundation for convergence lies in the recognition that certain reforms can generate contradictions within spectacular capitalism that open up spaces for more radical transformations. Antonio Gramsci's concept of "passive revolution" provides a framework for understanding how ruling classes can grant reforms that address popular demands while maintaining fundamental power relations (Gramsci, 1971). However,

Gramsci also emphasized that such reforms could create "cracks in the system" that revolutionary forces could exploit if they had adequate organization and strategy.

Contemporary theorists like John Holloway have developed similar arguments about "changing the world without taking power" through practices that create spaces of autonomy within capitalist systems (Holloway, 2002). This approach emphasizes prefigurative politics that embody alternative social relations rather than seeking to capture state power for revolutionary transformation.

The convergence analysis suggests that reformist proposals aligned with Situationist goals share several characteristics that enhance their transformative potential: they address fundamental aspects of commodification rather than just redistributing its benefits; they create material conditions for autonomous activity outside of market relations; they democratize control over strategic resources and institutions; and they challenge the temporal and spatial organization of spectacular capitalism. However, each of these reform areas also faces significant risks of recuperation that could turn potentially liberating initiatives into mechanisms for system maintenance. The spectacle's ability to absorb and neutralize potentially subversive forces remains a central challenge for any strategy that operates through institutional reform rather than revolutionary rupture.

Universal basic income exemplifies both the possibilities and limitations of reformist convergence with Situationist goals. While UBI could create material conditions to refuse wage labor and pursue autonomous activities, it could also serve as a minimal safety net that enables further commodification of social life and the retrenchment of more comprehensive social provisions. The key question is whether UBI implementation strengthens or weakens broader movements for economic democracy and cultural transformation.

Working time reduction similarly presents liberating possibilities and risks of recuperation. Fewer work hours could allow for non-commodified activities and collective experimentation, but they could also simply expand commodified leisure consumption or generate new forms of temporal discipline. The Situationist potential of working time reduction depends on its integration with cultural transformation that enables a creative use of liberated time.

Participatory urbanism demonstrates how spatial politics can challenge spectacular control while remaining vulnerable to cooptation by development interests and municipal authorities. Genuine participatory urbanism requires not just consultation but democratic control over investment decisions, land use planning, and urban development processes. The integration of spatial transformation with broader economic and cultural changes remains a significant challenge.

Democratic resource management shows perhaps the greatest potential for structural transformation by challenging capitalist control over strategic assets and investment decisions. However, democratic institutions operating within market systems face constant pressure to prioritize efficiency over social goals, while bureaucratic tendencies can reproduce hierarchical relations and technocratic decision-making.

The ecological crisis provides an additional impetus for convergence between Situationist critique and reformist proposals, as environmental limits increasingly expose the contradictions between capitalist accumulation and human survival. Climate change, biodiversity loss, and resource depletion require a rapid transformation of production and consumption patterns that may be impossible to achieve through market mechanisms alone (Foster, 2009).

The COVID-19 pandemic has demonstrated both the capacity for rapid institutional change when social priorities shift and the importance of public institutions and democratic resource management in addressing collective challenges. The pandemic response also revealed the limitations of market-oriented systems in providing essential services and sustaining social reproduction during crises.

Digital technologies create new possibilities for democratic participation and coordination that could facilitate convergence between Situationist goals and institutional reform. Online platforms can enable broader participation in planning processes, real-time feedback on policies, and new forms of cooperative organization that transcend geographical limitations. However, digital technologies also generate new forms of surveillance and control that require democratic responses (Zuboff, 2019).

The question of political strategy remains central to evaluating the possibilities of convergence. Reformist proposals require political coalitions and institutional capacity that may not exist or that may demand compromises that limit transformative potential. Revolutionary strategies face distinct challenges related to organization, consciousness, and the capacity for sustained struggle against entrenched power structures.

Recent social movements—including the alter-globalization protests, Occupy Wall Street, the Arab Spring, and various urban social movements—have experimented with prefigurative politics that embody alternative social relations while challenging existing power structures. These movements often combine immediate demands for reforms with broader visions of social transformation, suggesting possibilities for strategies that transcend traditional reform/revolution dichotomies (Graeber, 2009).

The success of such movements in achieving lasting transformations remains limited, reflecting both the power of existing institutions to resist change and the difficulty of scaling prefigurative practices to broader social transformation. The integration of prefigurative politics with institutional reform strategies may offer more promising approaches than either strategy alone.

Contemporary analysis suggests that convergence between Situationist critique and reformist proposals may be most viable when reforms are pursued as part of broader transformative strategies that include: cultural work to develop alternatives to consumerist lifestyles and spectacular relations; organizational development to strengthen democratic institutions and movement capacity; political education to foster critical consciousness about capitalism and its alternatives; and international solidarity to address the global character of capitalist domination.

The temporal dimension of transformation strategy deserves particular attention, given the SI's emphasis on revolutionary transformation and their skepticism toward gradual reform. However, the ecological crisis and other contemporary challenges may require a rapid transformation that combines institutional reform with cultural and organizational changes, rather than waiting for revolutionary opportunities that may not emerge in time to address ecological collapse.

2.4.6 *Contemporary Movements and Future Possibilities*

Contemporary social movements provide evidence of both the possibilities and limitations of the convergence between Situationist critique and reformist proposals. Movements for economic democracy, environmental justice, urban commons, and digital rights increasingly embody hybrid approaches that combine immediate demands for institutional reform with broader visions of social transformation that resonate with Situationist themes.

The global justice movement that emerged in the 1990s demonstrated possibilities for connecting local struggles with global critiques of capitalist development. Movements against corporate globalization combined opposition to specific trade agreements with broader visions of alternative economic relations based on solidarity, sustainability, and democratic participation rather than profit maximization (Notes from Nowhere, 2002).

These movements often employed tactics that evoked Situationist practices, including culture jamming, tactical media, and carnival-like protests that challenged spectacular representations while creating spaces for authentic encounters and collective creativity. The integration of cultural politics with economic critique reflected Situationist insights about the need to challenge capitalism at the level of everyday life, beyond just opposing its economic structures.

The Occupy movement, which emerged in the wake of the 2008 financial crisis, developed prefigurative approaches that combined immediate demands for economic reform with experimental practices that embodied alternative social relations. The Occupy encampments created temporary autonomous zones that challenged private property relations while experimenting with consensus decision-making, resource sharing, and non-hierarchical organization (Gitlin, 2012).

While Occupy achieved limited success in terms of specific policy demands, it significantly shifted public discourse on inequality and corporate power, inspiring organizing efforts on issues like debt resistance, housing justice, and public banking. The movement's emphasis on direct action and prefigurative politics reflected Situationist influences while adapting to contemporary conditions.

Urban social movements around the world have developed increasingly sophisticated approaches to spatial politics, which combine immediate demands for housing justice, public space access, and neighborhood preservation with broader visions of democratic urbanism. Barcelona En Comú, which grew out of housing rights activism to win municipal elections, demonstrates how local movements can scale prefigurative practices to institutional governance while maintaining grassroots participation (Russell, 2019).

The cooperative economy movement has grown significantly in recent years, encompassing worker cooperatives, housing cooperatives, platform cooperatives, and various forms of social enterprise that challenge capitalist property relations while operating within market systems. The Jackson

Rising movement in Mississippi shows how cooperative development can be integrated with broader strategies for community self-determination and economic democracy (Akuno & Nangwaya, 2017).

Environmental justice movements increasingly recognize the connections between the ecological crisis and economic democracy, developing approaches that integrate climate action with demands for worker ownership, community control of energy systems, and just transitions for fossil fuel-dependent communities. Green New Deal proposals in the United States and Europe reflect this integration, combining environmental protection with job creation and economic democratization (Pettifor, 2019).

Digital rights movements have emerged in response to surveillance capitalism and platform monopolies, developing alternatives based on commons governance, cooperative ownership, and democratic control of digital infrastructure. Platform cooperativism represents a significant development, creating cooperative alternatives to corporate platforms while retaining network effects and benefits for users (Scholz, 2016).

However, contemporary movements also face significant challenges that limit their transformative potential. The global dominance of capitalist markets generates competitive pressures that constrain alternative institutions; state power remains concentrated in institutions designed to serve capitalist accumulation; and cultural hegemony continues to naturalize market relations and consumer-oriented lifestyles. The rise of authoritarian populism in many countries demonstrates the spectacle's ability to channel popular discontent toward reactionary rather than liberating ends. Contemporary right-wing populisms can be interpreted, from a Situationist perspective, as spectacular responses to the contradictions of late capitalism, in which political antagonisms are increasingly mediated through images, narratives, and affective performances rather than collective projects of social transformation. This interpretation does not deny the importance of material grievances, institutional decay, or distributive conflict in the rise of contemporary right-wing populisms; rather, it highlights how such dynamics are mediated and amplified through spectacular forms that shape political subjectivity.

Right-wing movements have successfully appropriated critiques of elite power while directing anger toward scapegoated populations rather than structural transformation, illustrating the continuing importance of ideological struggle and cultural transformation.

Climate change generates an unprecedented urgency for social transformation while also revealing the limitations of existing institutions and strategies. The scale and speed of transformation required to avert catastrophic warming may outpace the capacity of gradual reform, while revolutionary strategies face the challenge of achieving rapid change without generating chaos that worsens the ecological crisis.

The COVID-19 pandemic has created additional challenges and opportunities for transformative movements. The economic disruption has intensified inequality and insecurity while demonstrating possibilities for rapid institutional shifts when social priorities change. The pandemic also revealed both the importance of public institutions and international cooperation and the limitations of market-oriented systems in addressing collective challenges.

The future possibilities of convergence between Situationist critique and reformist proposals may depend less on specific policy implementations than on their ability to create cultural and institutional conditions that allow for ongoing experimentation with alternative social relations. The SI's emphasis on the construction of situations remains relevant, not as a specific tactical approach, but as a strategic orientation toward creating spaces and opportunities for authentic encounters and collective creativity that can challenge spectacular relations and prefigure revolutionary transformation.

CHAPTER 3

Analytical Framework: Evaluating Reforms through Situationist Categories

To link Situationist critique with institutional analysis, this section develops a comprehensive evaluative framework that translates SI concepts into operational categories for assessing contemporary reforms. While concepts like "spectacle," "dérive," and "détournement" were developed within a revolutionary framework that explicitly rejected reformist politics, they offer powerful critical lenses for examining whether institutional reforms expand human autonomy and creativity or, inadvertently, reproduce the structures of alienation they aim to address (Debord, 1967; Vaneigem, 1967).

The development of this framework responds to a significant gap in contemporary policy analysis, which typically employs metrics derived from neoclassical economics or liberal political theory that may be inadequate for capturing the qualitative dimensions of human experience that were central to Situationist concerns. Traditional policy evaluation focuses on quantifiable outcomes like income distribution, employment rates, or service delivery efficiency, while neglecting questions about the nature of social relations, the quality of everyday experience, and the conditions for authentic human development (Sen, 1999).

The Situationist critique suggests that such conventional approaches may systematically miss the most important aspects of social transformation by focusing on distributive issues while ignoring the structural relations that shape human possibilities. From this perspective, reforms that

M. Brum, *Democratic Alternatives*,
https://doi.org/10.1007/978-3-032-23153-6_3

improve material conditions while leaving fundamental power relations intact may, in fact, strengthen rather than challenge systems of domination by making them more tolerable and legitimate (Marcuse, 1969).

Nevertheless, the framework developed here does not mechanically apply Situationist concepts to policy analysis. Rather, it seeks to translate core ideas about alienation, commodification, and authentic experience into analytical tools that can inform strategic thinking about social transformation, while remaining sensitive to the complex dynamics of institutional reform within capitalist societies.

The framework also recognizes that the conditions for applying Situationist analysis have changed significantly since the 1960s. Contemporary capitalism operates through more sophisticated mechanisms of social control and cultural management than those analyzed by Debord and Vaneigem, while new technologies, environmental crises, and forms of resistance generate both constraints and opportunities that were not present during the SI's historical moment (Boltanski & Chiapello, 2005; Harvey, 2005).

3.1 Framework Components and Methodological Considerations

The framework comprises five interrelated categories that, together, provide a comprehensive approach to evaluating the emancipatory potential of reforms: (1) spectacle and alienation, (2) decommodification and autonomy, (3) everyday life and play, (4) spatial reappropriation, and (5) détournement of institutions. Each category offers a specific lens for examining reforms while remaining alert to the risks of cooptation and the dynamic nature of social struggle.

These categories are not intended to be applied mechanically or independently but to inform a dialectical analysis that recognizes the contradictory nature of reform within capitalist systems. Reforms can simultaneously promote and limit human liberation, create new possibilities while foreclosing others, or may shift in their effects as they are contested and reappropriated by different social forces over time. The framework also incorporates insights from feminist theory, critical race theory, and postcolonial studies, which highlight dimensions of domination and liberation that were insufficiently addressed in the original Situationist analysis. Gender, race, and colonial relations fundamentally shape experiences of alienation and the possibilities for authentic activity in ways that require explicit attention, rather than assuming that class analysis alone can capture the full dynamics of social transformation (Federici, 2012; Gilmore, 2007).

Methodologically, the framework emphasizes the importance of participatory and ethnographic approaches that can capture qualitative dimensions of experience and social relations that quantitative metrics might miss. This includes attention to how reforms are experienced by different social groups, how they affect everyday life practices and social bonds, and how they create or constrain possibilities for collective agency and cultural transformation.

The framework also recognizes the temporal dimensions of reform evaluation, emphasizing that effects can change over time as reforms are implemented, contested, and adapted. Initial liberating potential may be limited by bureaucratic implementation, market pressures, or political backlash, while seemingly conservative reforms may generate unexpected openings for more radical transformation through unintended consequences or strategic appropriation by social movements.

3.1.1 *Spectacle and Alienation: Analyzing Mediation and Authentic Experience*

Debord's concept of the spectacle represents a totalizing social relationship in which lived experience becomes increasingly mediated by images, commodities, and representations, rather than arising from direct encounter and authentic activity (Debord, 1967). The spectacle is not merely a collection of media images or cultural products but a fundamental transformation in social relations that separates individuals from their own activity and from genuine encounter with others.

Evaluating reforms through this lens requires developing sophisticated analytical tools to distinguish between changes that intensify passive consumption and commodification and those that generate genuine openings for active participation and authentic experience. This analysis must avoid both crude oppositions between "authentic" and "inauthentic" experience and naive assumptions that any reduction in market relations automatically enhances human freedom.

The spectacle operates through multiple mechanisms that reforms could either challenge or reinforce: the separation of producers from consumers; the transformation of social relations into commodity exchange; the mediation of experience through professional expertise and bureaucratic procedures; the substitution of active creation with passive consumption; and the colonization of the imagination by commercial and political representations (Vaneigem, 1967).

For example, a Universal Basic Income program that simply subsidizes consumer demand without altering power relations over production, culture, or political decision-making could reinforce the logic of the spectacle by enabling expanded consumption while maintaining the separation between production and consumption decisions. Beneficiaries might have greater purchasing power but would remain excluded from decisions about what is produced, how it is produced, and for what purposes.

In contrast, a UBI program that is combined with the expansion of cooperative enterprises, community-controlled media, and participatory decision-making institutions could disrupt the spectacle's logic by enabling people to refuse alienated labor and pursue autonomous projects that integrate creative activity with social participation. The key difference lies not in the cash transfer itself but in its relationship to broader institutional and cultural transformation.

Metrics for evaluating spectacle and alienation could include: changes in the proportion of time spent in passive versus active roles; the degree of individuals' participation in decisions that affect their everyday lives; the diversity and accessibility of cultural production and distribution; the degree of separation between mental and manual labor, production and consumption, individual and collective activity; and subjective reports on meaning, creativity, and social connection in daily activities.

This category connects with broader debates in critical theory about "authentic" versus "false" needs, drawing especially on Herbert Marcuse's analysis of how advanced capitalism generates artificial needs that serve system maintenance rather than human development (Marcuse, 1969). However, the framework attempts to avoid paternalistic judgments about consumption choices by focusing on the structural conditions that enable or constrain authentic self-determination, rather than prescribing particular lifestyles.

The analysis of spectacle and alienation also requires attention to how reforms affect the experiences of mediation and authenticity for different social groups. Women's experiences of spectacular relations may differ significantly from men's due to gendered divisions of labor and cultural representations; racial minorities may face particular forms of exclusion and stereotyping; and class positions may shape both exposure to spectacular relations and the capacity to resist them (Davis, 1981; hooks, 1994).

Contemporary developments in digital technology, surveillance capitalism, and platform-mediated social relations generate new forms of spectacular mediation that were not present during the SI's historical moment but that extend and intensify the dynamics they analyzed (Zuboff, 2019; Srnicek, 2017). Reforms must be evaluated for their effects on these new forms of spectacle as well as on the traditional forms the SI originally critiqued.

The temporal dimension of spectacular relations also requires attention, as reforms may have different effects on the reproduction of the spectacle over time. Initial disruptions of the spectacular logic may be recuperated through market adaptation, cultural appropriation, or bureaucratic routinization, while reforms that initially appear to reinforce spectacular relations may generate unforeseen openings for more authentic activity through their effects on material conditions or social organization.

3.1.2 Decommodification and Autonomy: Beyond Market Dependence

Building on Gøsta Esping-Andersen's influential concept of decommodification, this category examines the extent to which reforms allow individuals and communities to secure livelihoods and pursue meaningful activities outside the strictures of labor markets and commodity relations (Esping-Andersen, 1990). However, the framework extends Esping-Andersen's primarily economic focus to encompass broader questions of autonomy, creativity, and self-determination that were central to the Situationist analysis.

Decommodification, in the Situationist sense, involves not just providing alternative sources of income or services but creating conditions that reduce the extent to which human relations, creative activity, and social reproduction are organized through market mechanisms. This includes attention to time, space, and cultural resources, as well as material resources, and emphasizes collective as well as individual dimensions of autonomy.

For the Situationist International, the crucial question is whether reforms create the material and cultural conditions to refuse alienated labor and embrace what Vaneigem termed "life" versus "survival"—the difference between creative self-realization and mere biological reproduction (Vaneigem, 1967). This requires examining not just sources of income but also the availability of time, access to common resources, cultural support for non-market activities, and opportunities for collective creativity and social experimentation.

Universal Basic Income, universal public services, working time reduction, and democratic resource management can all be evaluated for their ability to reduce market dependence and expand autonomy. However, the effects of such reforms depend heavily on their design, scale, and integration with broader institutional and cultural changes, rather than on their formal characteristics alone.

A robust analysis of decommodification and autonomy must consider multiple dimensions: material autonomy (access to the resources needed for a dignified survival independent of market income); temporal autonomy (control over the allocation of time and the rhythm of life, rather than being subordinated to employer or bureaucratic schedules); spatial autonomy (access to spaces for activity and creativity that are not subject to market or state control); cultural autonomy (the ability to participate in cultural creation, rather than being limited to consuming commodified culture); and political autonomy (participation in collective decision-making about resource allocation and social priorities).

Indicators for evaluating decommodification and autonomy could include: the proportion of individual and household income that comes from sources other than wage labor; time available for discretionary activities not dictated by market or bureaucratic imperatives; access to common resources like public spaces, cultural facilities, natural environments, and shared infrastructure; rates of participation in cooperative enterprises, community organizations, and cultural creation; subjective measures of control over everyday life and work; and evidence of collective capacity to make democratic decisions about resource use and social priorities.

The gendered dimensions of decommodification require particular attention, as women's economic dependence has historically taken different forms from men's, including dependence on male wages rather than direct market participation, unpaid responsibility for social reproduction activities, and exclusion from many forms of autonomous economic activity (Fraser, 1994). Reforms that increase formal labor market participation without addressing gendered divisions of unpaid labor may actually increase rather than decrease women's dependence and workload.

Similarly, the racial and colonial dimensions of commodification generate specific forms of exclusion and exploitation that reforms must explicitly address, rather than assuming that general decommodification will automatically benefit all social groups equally. The historical use of racial classification to exclude groups from wage labor, property ownership, and political participation creates ongoing dynamics that shape contemporary experiences of market dependence and autonomy (Robinson, 2000).

The collective dimensions of autonomy deserve emphasis, as they distinguish Situationist approaches from liberal concepts of individual freedom. The SI emphasized that authentic autonomy arises through social relations and collective activity, rather than individual isolation. Therefore, reforms must be evaluated for their effects on social solidarity, the collective capacity for self-organization, and community control over shared resources and institutions.

Contemporary debates on commons governance, community economies, and the solidarity economy provide valuable frameworks for thinking through collective autonomy that expand on Situationist insights and address practical questions about institutional design and sustainability (Ostrom, 1990; Gibson-Graham et al., 2013). These approaches emphasize the importance of democratic participation in economic decision-making and the creation of institutions that support mutual aid and resource sharing.

The relationship between decommodification and ecological sustainability also requires attention, as reforms that simply enable expanded consumption of commodified goods and services may reproduce environmental destruction even while reducing direct market dependence. Genuine decommodification may require shifts toward less resource-intensive forms of social organization and cultural activity that prioritize intrinsic values over exchange values (Jackson, 2017).

3.1.3 *Everyday Life, Desire, and Play: Transforming Daily Experience*

Raoul Vaneigem's emphasis on liberating everyday life from bureaucratic control and commodified relations forms the basis of this analytical category, which examines how reforms affect the qualitative dimensions of daily experience that conventional policy analysis often neglects (Vaneigem, 1967). The framework asks whether reforms simply redistribute resources or whether they expand the capacity for joyful, creative, and playful practices that resist the reduction of life to mere survival and accumulation.

This category requires attention to the phenomenological dimensions of social transformation—how reforms feel to those who experience them and what they enable in terms of emotional, creative, and relational potentialities. Such an analysis necessarily involves qualitative research methods, including ethnography, participatory research, and life history approaches, that can capture the texture of lived experience rather than its mere statistical aggregates (Lefebvre, 1991a).

The Situationist concept of "play" provides a crucial lens for this analysis, though it must be differentiated from both commercial entertainment and institutionally organized recreational activities. For the SI, play represented a form of creative activity that was freely chosen, intrinsically motivated, experimental in character, and oriented toward the creation of new situations rather than predetermined outcomes (Huizinga, 1955).

Vaneigem's critique of "survival" versus "life" emphasized that capitalist social organization reduces human activity to the reproduction of existing conditions rather than enabling the creation of new possibilities. Everyday life under capitalism is organized around routine, habit, and the fulfillment of externally imposed demands, rather than around the exploration of desire and the realization of creative potential. The liberation of everyday life therefore requires not just changes in institutional structures but a transformation in the rhythm, content, and meaning of daily activities. This could involve: greater flexibility in the use of time and scheduling; opportunities for creative expression and experimentation; spaces and resources for social interaction and collective activity; a reduction in bureaucratic requirements and professional mediation; and cultural support for activities pursued for intrinsic rather than instrumental reasons.

Examples of how this category might be applied include: examining how working time reduction affects family relations, creative pursuits, community participation, and personal development; analyzing how participatory budgeting influences civic culture, social bonds, and the capacity for collective problem-solving; investigating how cooperative ownership modifies workplace relations, job satisfaction, and opportunities for skill development and creative input; or studying how community land trusts affect neighborhood social dynamics, resident empowerment, and cultural activity.

The framework emphasizes that such effects cannot be assumed from the formal characteristics of the policy but must be investigated empirically through methods that capture participants' understandings of their own experiences. The same policy intervention may have vastly different effects on everyday life depending on the implementation processes, cultural contexts, and the broader constellation of social relations in which it operates.

The category also requires attention to how desire is shaped and expressed under different social conditions. The Situationist analysis suggested that capitalist social organization systematically distorts desire by channeling it toward the consumption of commodities and competitive individualism, rather than creative expression and social connection (Marcuse, 1955). Therefore, reforms must be evaluated for their effects on the quality and direction of desire, as well as their ability to satisfy expressed desires.

This analysis must avoid both romantic assumptions about "natural" human desires that exist independently of social conditions and cynical dismissal of popular desires as mere products of manipulation. Instead, the framework examines how different institutional arrangements enable or constrain the development of desires oriented toward human flourishing rather than system reproduction.

The relationship between the individual and collective dimensions of desire requires particular attention, as the SI emphasized that authentic desire emerges through social relations rather than individual isolation. Therefore, reforms must be evaluated for their effects on social bonds, community formation, and the collective capacity for cultural creation, as well as their effects on individual well-being and satisfaction.

Gender, race, and class dynamics fundamentally shape experiences of everyday life and the possibilities for liberation, in ways that require explicit analytical attention. Women's everyday life has historically been organized around unpaid care work and domestic responsibilities, which may limit opportunities for autonomous activity even when formal barriers are removed. Similarly, racial subordination and class exploitation generate specific constraints on everyday life that reforms must explicitly address, rather than assuming that general improvements will automatically benefit all groups equally.

Contemporary developments in digital technology, urban design, and work organization create new possibilities and constraints for the transformation of everyday life that go beyond those analyzed in original Situationist theory. Therefore, the framework must be adaptive to emerging conditions while maintaining a focus on core questions about creativity, autonomy, and authentic social relations.

3.1.4 Spatial Reappropriation and Urban Commons: Cities as Sites of Liberation

The Situationist International's critique of functionalist urbanism and their experimental practice of the *dérive* highlight urban space as a crucial field of emancipatory possibility, making spatial analysis essential to evaluating contemporary reforms (Sadler, 1998). This category examines whether reforms reproduce commodified urban forms that separate life into functional zones of work, residence, and consumption, or whether they enable collective spatial reappropriation for encounter, play, and experimentation.

Drawing on Henri Lefebvre's influential concept of the "right to the city," the framework analyzes the spatial dimensions of reforms not just as technical questions of service delivery or land-use efficiency but as fundamental questions about who controls urban space and for what purposes (Lefebvre, 1968). This includes not only formal planning processes but also how reforms affect everyday spatial practices, mobility patterns, public space accessibility, and opportunities for experimentation and collective appropriation of space.

The Situationist critique of urban planning emphasized that the spatial organization of cities reflects and reproduces broader social relations of domination. Modernist urbanism's division of cities into separate zones for different activities—residential suburbs, commercial districts, industrial areas, entertainment zones—parallels and reinforces the spectacle's separation of life into discrete and specialized spheres that prevent an integrated human development (Debord, 1967).

Contemporary urban development continues these patterns through processes of gentrification that displace working-class communities to make way for commercial development and middle-class consumption; suburban sprawl that increases car dependence and reduces opportunities for spontaneous social encounter; public space privatization that subjects urban life to commercial control; and security measures that criminalize non-commercial uses of urban space (Harvey, 2012).

Reforms can be evaluated for their ability to challenge or reproduce these spatial patterns using multiple indicators: levels of citizen participation in planning processes; accessibility, quality, and diversity of uses of public space; community control over local resources and land-use decisions; evidence of experimental spatial practices and temporary appropriations; residential stability and protection against displacement; integration of different activities and social groups within neighborhoods; and support for non-commercial cultural and social activities in public space. The framework also examines how reforms affect what Lefebvre termed "differential space"—spaces of difference, encounter, and creative appropriation that resist reduction to exchange value and functional efficiency (Lefebvre, 1991b).

Such spaces could include community gardens, cooperative housing, social centers, maker spaces, and other facilities that enable collective activity and cultural creation rather than mere individual consumption.

Participatory urbanism initiatives provide important examples of spatial reappropriation that can be analyzed through this framework. Community land trusts take land out of speculation while enabling democratic governance of neighborhood development; participatory budgeting gives residents direct control over public investment in infrastructure and services; tactical urbanism interventions demonstrate alternative uses of streets and public spaces; and community-led development prioritizes affordable housing and local businesses over gentrification and displacement.

However, such initiatives also face significant limitations and risks of cooptation that must be critically analyzed. Market pressures, real estate speculation, and regulatory frameworks often constrain participatory possibilities, while successful neighborhood improvements may increase property values and contribute to the displacement of existing residents. The challenge is to identify conditions under which participatory urbanism can build community power and resist commodification, rather than just managing its social consequences.

The global dimension of urban development also requires attention, as local spatial struggles are increasingly connected to international circuits of capital investment, policy transfer, and cultural influence. Therefore, the framework must consider how reforms affect the integration of cities into global hierarchies and their capacity to resist external pressures that limit local democracy and spatial experimentation.

Climate change generates additional imperatives and opportunities for spatial reappropriation, as cities must rapidly reduce carbon emissions and adapt to environmental changes. Community-controlled renewable energy systems, urban agriculture, green infrastructure, and climate adaptation measures could increase local autonomy while addressing environmental challenges, but they could also be implemented in ways that reinforce existing inequalities and exclusions.

The relationship between spatial transformation and broader social change requires careful analysis, as spatial improvements alone cannot address the underlying economic and political structures that produce urban inequality and commodification. Therefore, the framework examines how spatial reforms connect with broader strategies for economic democracy, cultural transformation, and political empowerment, rather than treating spatial change as an end in itself.

3.1.5 *Détournement of Institutions: Subverting Dominant Logic from Within*

The Situationist practice of *détournement*—the appropriation and subversion of existing cultural forms to expose their ideological function and redirect them toward revolutionary ends—can be extended as an evaluative category to analyze institutions and reforms themselves (Debord & Wolman, 1956). This category examines whether reforms are assimilated into the dominant logic of the spectacle or whether they succeed in subverting that logic from within, creating new possibilities for democratic participation and social experimentation that exceed their original design.

The concept of institutional *détournement* recognizes that the meaning and effects of reforms are not determined solely by their formal characteristics but emerge through processes of political struggle, cultural interpretation, and practical implementation that can transform their original purposes. The same policy—such as participatory budgeting, universal basic income, or the development of cooperative enterprises—could function as a technocratic legitimation of austerity and inequality, or as a collective empowerment that redefines social priorities and challenges existing power relations.

This analytical approach emphasizes the contested nature of reforms and the importance of political strategy in determining their transformative potential. Rather than treating reforms as fixed objects with predetermined effects, the framework examines how they become sites of struggle between different social forces with competing visions for social organization and human possibility.

Successful institutional *détournement* could involve: appropriating reforms de-signed to maintain the system and redirecting them toward more radical ends; using institutional resources to build capacity for broader social transformation; creating spaces within institutions for experimental practices that prefigure alternative social relations; linking institutional reforms with movement organizing and cultural transformation; and developing analyses and strategies that reveal contradictions within existing institutions while pointing toward more fundamental alternatives.

For example, participatory budgeting initiatives that were originally designed to manage fiscal austerity and legitimize public spending cuts could be *détourned* by community organizations to build collective capacity for economic planning, develop alternative priorities for resource allocation, and create models of broader democratic control over investment decisions. The key is whether such initiatives remain within the boundaries set by their original design or generate dynamics that exceed and challenge them.

Similarly, worker cooperative development programs, designed to offer entrepreneurial opportunities to displaced workers, could be appropriated by labor movements to more broadly challenge capitalist property relations, develop solidarity economy networks that operate on principles other than capitalist market ones, and create institutional bases for broader working-class organization and political education.

The evaluation of institutional *détournement* requires attention to multiple dimensions: the degree to which reforms create opportunities for democratic participation that did not previously exist; whether they enable participants to develop new capacities for collective self-organization and critical analysis; how they affect relations between different social groups and challenges to existing hierarchies; their integration with broader social movements and cultural transformation efforts; and their potential to prefigure and build toward more comprehensive social transformation.

This analysis must avoid both naive optimism about the transformative potential of reforms and cynical dismissal of all institutional engagement as inevitably cooptive. Instead, the framework offers tools for a strategic analysis that can guide decisions about when and how to engage with institutional reforms as part of broader transformative strategies.

The temporal dimension of institutional *détournement* requires particular attention, as the effects of reforms may change over time as they are implemented, contested, and adapted by different social forces. Initial subversive potential may be limited by bureaucratic routinization, market pressures, or political backlash, while reforms that initially serve system-maintenance functions may generate unexpected openings for more radical transformation through their effects on consciousness, organization, or material conditions.

The framework also recognizes that institutional *détournement* requires complementary cultural and organizational work that cannot be achieved through policy reform alone. Subverting institutional logic requires alternative visions, values, and practices that can guide reappropriation efforts and resist pressures for cooptation. This cultural dimension connects the institutional analysis to broader questions about ideology, consciousness, and social movement strategy.

The global dimension of institutional transformation also requires attention, as local reforms operate within broader systems of economic, political, and cultural power that may limit their subversive potential. Therefore, the framework examines how local experiments in institutional *détournement* connect with broader networks of resistance and alternative development that can provide mutual support and strategic coordination across different scales and contexts.

3.2 Operationalization Matrix for Situationist-Informed Policy Evaluation

The following matrix provides a structured approach to evaluating public policies through the five analytical categories developed in this framework. It examines both the intrinsic characteristics of policies and their contextual conditions of emergence, maintenance, and potential for preserving achievements even after institutional discontinuation.

3.2.1 Analytical Notes

From a Situationist perspective, the transformative potential of public policies is contingent upon their capacity to engage with all five evaluative dimensions—spectacle and alienation, decommodification and autonomy, everyday life and play, spatial reappropriation, and détournement of institutions. Policies that address these dimensions in a coherent and integrated manner are more likely to produce systemic change, rather than isolated or symbolic effects. Conversely, policies that neglect certain dimensions may inadvertently reinforce existing structures of alienation and passivity.

Guy Debord's concept of the "spectacle" refers to the commodification of social life and the passive consumption of images and representations. In *The Society of the Spectacle*, Debord argues that "all that once was directly lived has become mere representation" Debord (1967). Policies that fail to challenge the spectacle risk perpetuating a society where individuals are spectators rather than active participants in their own lives. For instance, initiatives that promote consumerism under the guise of cultural enrichment may inadvertently reinforce the very alienation they seek to mitigate (Table 3.1).

Moreover, the conditions of possibility for the emergence of policies are as critical as the policies themselves. Even the most radical policy designs can falter if they are not situated within supportive political, economic, or cultural contexts. For example, a policy aimed at decommodifying essential

Table 3.1 Operationalization matrix for situationist-informed policy evaluation

Evaluative Dimension	*(1) Spectacle and Alienation*	*(2) Decommodification and autonomy*	*(3) Everyday life and play*	*(4) Spatial reappropriation*	*(5) Détournement of institutions*
Policy Objectives / target population	Does the policy challenge mediated representation or reinforce passive consumption?	Does it reduce market dependence and expand autonomous decision-making?	Does it create conditions for creative, playful activities beyond survival?	Does it enable collective spatial appropriation and experimentation?	Does it subvert institutional logic toward democratic participation?
Conditions of possibility	Presence of critical social movements; cultural openness to anti-spectacular critique	Labor organization strength; fiscal capacity for decommodification	Cultural infrastructure for non-commodified leisure; educational support	Participatory planning frameworks; commons governance traditions	Political opportunity structures; elite divisions; institutional flexibility
Conditions of maintenance	Ongoing cultural work challenging dominant representations	Sustained political coalitions defending non-market provisioning	Intergenerational transmission of alternative values and practices	Community control over development decisions; protection from gentrification	Active social movements preventing bureaucratization and cooptation
Capacity to Preserve achievements if policy is suppressed	Cultural shifts in consciousness and desire that outlast formal programs	Established rights and expectations that resist rollback	Embodied practices and skills that persist informally	Transformed spatial relationships and community networks	Organizational capacity and democratic skills developed through participation

services may be ineffective without a robust labor movement, sufficient fiscal resources, and political will. Conversely, even modest policies can have profound transformative effects when the conditions of possibility—such as strong grassroots movements or institutional flexibility—are favorable.

The matrix also facilitates the identification of synergies across policies and contexts. Transformative outcomes often emerge from conjunctive effects, where multiple policies are implemented in parallel or in mutually reinforcing ways. For example, reducing working hours while simultaneously funding creative leisure programs does more than improve well-being; it reshapes everyday life, encourages autonomous decision-making, and builds cultural capacities that resist commodification. This underscores the importance of a holistic, systems-oriented approach to policy design that treats social transformation as a cumulative process rather than a series of isolated interventions.

Finally, the matrix emphasizes the importance of considering the durability of policy achievements. Even if a policy is dismantled, its transformative potential can persist if it succeeds in producing cultural shifts, establishing entrenched rights, or embedding alternative practices within everyday life. This highlights the need for policy evaluation frameworks that extend beyond immediate outputs to consider long-term processes of social change.

3.2.2 *Strategic Implications*

The operationalization matrix suggests that policy selection should not be guided by a unitary criterion based solely on isolated effectiveness or efficiency. Instead, it advocates for a conjunctive criterion, where the value of a policy is assessed in relation to other policies and the broader socio-political context. This requires moving away from linear, single-policy evaluation toward a systemic perspective, where policies are understood as part of an interconnected web of interventions that collectively shape social transformation.

Strategically, this implies that policymakers should prioritize policy mixes that maximize articulation across the five dimensions, rather than seeking single "silver bullet" solutions. For instance, policies aimed at expanding autonomy without addressing cultural conditions of spectacle and alienation are unlikely to produce deep change. Similarly, spatial reappropriation efforts divorced from democratic institution-building risk producing ephemeral gains that are easily reversed. A conjunctive criterion, therefore, encourages integrated policy strategies that deliberately combine complementary interventions—such as participatory governance, cultural programs, and economic reforms—to create conditions for sustained transformation.

Another significant strategic implication concerns the resilience of policy achievements. Policies should be designed not only for their immediate effects but for their capacity to create self-reinforcing dynamics that endure beyond their formal implementation. This requires embedding mechanisms for intergenerational transmission of values, cultivating cultural infrastructures that support non-commodified life, and fostering organizational capacities within communities. Strategic planning, thus, must incorporate both short-term feasibility and long-term sustainability, recognizing that transformative change emerges from processes that unfold over years or decades.

Finally, the matrix underscores that the effectiveness of a policy is inherently relational: it depends on the interplay between the policy itself, other simultaneous or antecedent policies, and the socio-political context. This relational understanding implies that policy evaluation and selection should be iterative, adaptive, and context-sensitive, enabling policymakers to respond to changing conditions, emerging challenges, and opportunities for synergies. In other words, the matrix invites a strategic approach to policy design that treats transformation as an ongoing, conjunctive process rather than a fixed, one-off outcome.

3.3 Application Methodology and Research Strategies

The application of this analytical framework requires methodological approaches that can capture both the quantitative and qualitative dimensions of social transformation while remaining sensitive to the perspectives and experiences of those most directly affected by reforms. This section outlines research strategies that can operationalize the framework's categories while maintaining a commitment to participatory and democratic approaches to knowledge production.

The framework's emphasis on the transformation of everyday life, authentic experience, and collective agency requires research methods that allow access to the subjective dimensions of experience, avoiding both individualistic reductionism and romantic assumptions about popular consciousness. Ethnographic approaches, life history methods, participatory action research, and community-based research partnerships provide tools for understanding how reforms affect lived experience while building relationships with communities engaged in struggles for social transformation.

Quantitative analysis remains important for documenting distributive effects, institutional changes, and broad social patterns, but it must be complemented with qualitative approaches that can capture the dimensions of meaning, relation, and process that statistics alone do not reveal. Mixed-methods approaches, which combine different types of data and analysis, can provide a more comprehensive understanding of the complex and contradictory effects of reforms.

The framework also emphasizes the importance of longitudinal analysis that allows for tracking changes in the effects of reforms over time as they are implemented, contested, and adapted. Comparative case analysis can illuminate how similar reforms produce different outcomes under different conditions, helping to identify the factors that enhance or constrain their transformative capacity.

Participatory evaluation approaches, which involve affected communities in defining success criteria, collecting data, and interpreting results, can ensure that the analysis remains rooted in lived experience while strengthening the capacity for ongoing strategic reflection and organizational development. Such approaches align with the Situationist commitment to demystifying expertise and democratizing knowledge production.

3.4 Methodological Considerations

This framework requires multi-method approaches that combine quantitative evaluation, ethnographic research, and critical-theoretical analysis. Quantitative methods can measure the material effects of reforms on income, work time, and access to resources. Ethnographic approaches capture lived experiences and cultural dimensions. Critical analysis interprets these findings through Situationist categories, avoiding both uncritical celebration and total rejection of institutional possibilities.

Methodologically, this implies a commitment to what Creswell and Creswell (2017) terms a *mixed-methods design*, where the integration of numerical indicators and qualitative narratives offers a more complete picture of social change than either alone. Quantitative strategies are essential for establishing the scope and magnitude of reforms: microsimulation models, econometric estimations, and impact evaluations can identify how redistributive policies, work-time reductions, or access to common resources reconfigure social stratification (Atkinson, 2015; Bourguignon et al., 2015). These techniques provide empirical evidence on the reforms' capacity to alter material conditions, a prerequisite for evaluating their emancipatory potential.

However, numerical indicators are insufficient for capturing the dimensions of alienation and everyday creativity that the Situationists emphasized (De Beistegui & Ross, 2018). Ethnographic and qualitative methods therefore play a crucial role. Participant observation, interviews, and narrative analysis can reveal how people and communities experience reforms in practice, particularly concerning leisure, autonomy, and the reappropriation of daily life. As illustrated by Willis (1977) and Hochschild (2012), cultural and subjective accounts of social policy often show dimensions invisible to purely statistical measures. Ethnography thus allows the research to remain attentive to the lived contradictions between formal institutional change and the persistence of alienated social relations.

Critical-theoretical analysis provides the bridge between empirical findings and Situationist categories like *recuperation*, *spectacle*, and *dérive*. Instead of reading policies as either inherently emancipatory or inevitably coopted, this dimension situates them within the dialectic of political struggle and cultural transformation (Debord, 1995; Plant, 1992). It highlights how institutional changes can simultaneously open up new possibilities for collective action and be subject to recuperation processes that neutralize their radical potential. This perspective aligns with critical traditions in political economy that see reforms as terrains of struggle rather than technical solutions (Fraser, 2013; Polanyi, 2001a).

The framework emphasizes process over outcomes, recognizing that the emancipatory potential of reforms depends on ongoing political struggle and cultural development, rather than on technical design alone. As Wright (2010a) argues, institutional innovations like universal basic income or work-time reduction must be understood not as final solutions but as potential *real utopias*: institutional arrangements that prefigure broader transformations, even while remaining embedded in conflictual contexts. This perspective rejects the illusion of neutrality in technical design and foregrounds the centrality of collective appropriation and democratic practice.

Finally, the framework recognizes that Situationist goals cannot be achieved by institutional reforms alone, but they can be advanced by those that create favorable conditions for broader social transformation.

For example, policies that reduce economic precarity or expand free time may not directly abolish the spectacle, but they may generate material and cultural spaces where new forms of subjectivity and collective experimentation become possible (Gorz, 1999; Harvey, 2000). The methodological implication is to evaluate reforms not merely in terms of efficiency or equity but on their capacity to nurture the conditions for lived critique and transformative praxis.

CHAPTER 4

Case Studies

4.1 Iceland's Working Time Reduction Experiment (2015–2019)

4.1.1 Background and Design

Between 2015 and 2019, Iceland conducted two large-scale trials of working time reduction encompassing approximately 2500 workers—about 1.5% of the national workforce. The experiments, jointly organized by the City of Reykjavík, the national government, and various trade unions, tested the feasibility of reducing the standard workweek from 40 to 35–36 hours without a cut in pay (Haraldsson & Kellam, 2021).

The theoretical foundation for these experiments drew on decades of research on work-life balance, productivity theory, and the economics of time allocation (Golden, 2012a). Building on previous pilot experiences in Sweden and Belgium, the Icelandic approach was distinguished by its comprehensive scope and systematic evaluation methodology (Hayden, 2006). The experiments were explicitly framed within Iceland's broader commitment to gender equality and work-life balance, reflecting Nordic social-democratic values that prioritize collective well-being alongside economic efficiency (Esping-Andersen, 1990).

The trials were not randomized controlled experiments but naturalistic field studies implemented across diverse sectors, including municipal

M. Brum, *Democratic Alternatives*,
https://doi.org/10.1007/978-3-032-23153-6_4

offices, hospitals, schools, social services, prisons, and childcare centers. This sectoral diversity was crucial for testing the generalizability of working time reduction across different types of work—from care services that require continuous coverage to knowledge work that allows for greater scheduling flexibility (Lehndorff, 2014). Each workplace developed specific strategies to maintain productivity through task reorganization, meeting rationalization, flexible scheduling, better use of technology, and workflow optimization (Stronge, 2019).

The experiments were evaluated using mixed-methods approaches that combined surveys, interviews, focus groups, and productivity metrics collected before, during, and after implementation. This comprehensive evaluation design reflected action-research methodologies that emphasize participatory knowledge creation and iterative policy learning (Reason & Bradbury, 2008). The research framework also incorporated indicators of well-being, environmental impact assessments, and broader social effects, moving beyond narrow measures of productivity to capture multiple dimensions of policy success (Fioramonti, 2017).

This design aligns with broader traditions of action-research and workplace democracy experiments in Northern Europe, particularly the Swedish work environment reforms of the 1970s and Norwegian industrial democracy programs (Koslowski et al., 2022; Meil & Henselek, 2017). The participatory approach to policy experimentation reflects what Unger (2019) terms "democratic experimentalism": the systematic use of small-scale trials to test and refine larger institutional changes.

4.1.2 Key Findings

The evaluation revealed consistently positive outcomes across multiple dimensions, challenging conventional assumptions about the relationship between productivity and work hours. Workers reported significant improvements in work-life balance: 41% indicated better reconciliation and 71% reported reduced burnout (Haraldsson & Kellam, 2021). Stress-related symptoms decreased notably, with improvements in sleep quality, physical health indicators, and mental well-being measures. These findings align with extensive research on work stress and its health consequences (Siegrist & Li, 2017; Bakker & Demerouti, 2014).

Importantly, productivity remained stable or improved in most participating organizations, contradicting neoclassical assumptions that shorter hours would proportionally reduce output. Productivity gains resulted from several mechanisms: reduced fatigue leading to better work quality, elimination of non-essential activities, increased concentration in reduced hours, and higher employee motivation and engagement (Pencavel, 2015). These findings support "efficiency wage" theories, which suggest that improvements in worker well-being can offset the reduction in hours through increased productivity (Akerlof, 1986).

The experiments also generated broader institutional effects beyond the direct participants. Following the trials' success, collective bargaining agreements extended the right to request shorter hours to approximately 85% of the Icelandic workforce by 2021. This rapid scalability reflects the strength of Iceland's coordinated bargaining system and the broad political consensus around work-life balance priorities (Berg et al., 2021). The scaling-up process is reminiscent of Nordic traditions of integrating experimental policy innovations into universal labor regimes through "policy learning" mechanisms (Brandt & Schulten, 2019; Brandt et al., 2021).

The implications for gender equality were particularly significant, addressing long-standing feminist critiques of standard working arrangements. The reduction in hours enabled a more equitable distribution of care work between partners, with men increasing their participation in childcare and domestic responsibilities by an average of 23 minutes per day (Haraldsson & Kellam, 2021). Women reported a reduction in "time poverty" and a better ability to combine paid work with family responsibilities. This finding aligns with feminist arguments that working time reduction could address the "double burden" issues faced by women in the labor market (Folbre, 2001; Hempel, 2022).

Environmental effects, while not systematically measured, showed promising indicators. Reduced commuting decreased transport-related carbon emissions, and survey responses suggested shifts toward more sustainable consumption patterns with increased free time (Fitzgerald & Wray, 2019). Some participants reported growing their own food, reducing convenience-product consumption, and engaging in more local community activities—patterns consistent with degrowth theories that link time affluence with ecological sustainability (Kallis, 2018).

The policy also demonstrated significant fiscal benefits for public sector employers. Reduced sick leave, lower staff turnover, and improved service quality offset the costs of maintaining salary levels despite the reduction in hours. Healthcare costs decreased as worker well-being improved, generating broader social savings (Coote et al., 2021). These findings challenge narrow cost-benefit analyses that focus solely on immediate labor costs without considering broader social and economic effects.

4.1.3 Situationist Analysis

Applying the five-category framework reveals both the emancipatory potential and limitations of the Icelandic experience, illustrating the complex relationship between policy reforms and radical social transformation.

Spectacle and Alienation: The reduction in working time generated measurable increases in discretionary time and reductions in work-related stress, partially challenging what Debord (1967) termed the "colonization of time" by capitalist work rhythms. Workers reported greater capacity to engage in non-market activities—family time, creative projects, community participation, and rest—that resist the total subsumption of life to labor (Weeks, 2011). The policy challenged dominant narratives that equate longer hours with productivity and value, creating space for alternative valuations of time use (Southerton, 2003).

However, the increase in free time does not automatically escape commodified consumption patterns without complementary cultural shifts. Many participants still experienced pressures to fill the new time with consumption activities rather than developing what Vaneigem (2012) termed "authentic desires" (Schor, 2010). The persistence of consumer culture suggests that the liberation of time, on its own, is insufficient to overcome the spectacle without broader cultural transformation that addresses the commodification of desire itself.

Decommodification and Autonomy: By maintaining wages while reducing hours, the policy increased workers' temporal autonomy without creating new dependencies on welfare systems. This represents a partial decommodification on the temporal dimension, following Esping-Andersen (1990)'s framework for understanding welfare state interventions in market relations. Workers gained greater capacity to refuse overtime, negotiate flexible arrangements, and redistribute time toward care, community, and personal projects (Coote et al., 2021).

The policy reinforced what Rosa (2019) terms "temporal sovereignty": the capacity to control the allocation of time based on personal values rather than external market imperatives. Nevertheless, workers remained fundamentally dependent on wage income from employers, and the policy did not challenge deeper structures of workplace hierarchy or capitalist ownership. The reform represents, in this sense, what Gorz (1999) characterized as a "politics of time" within capitalist structures rather than a fundamental transformation of production relations.

Everyday Life and Play: The qualitative evidence indicated an expansion of opportunities for family time, hobbies, rest, and community engagement—conditions conducive to Vaneigem (2012)'s vision of a liberated everyday life. Participants reported more spontaneous social interactions, creative activities, and unstructured time that allowed for what the Situationists termed "constructed situations": moments of authentic experience outside of commodity relations (Plant, 1992).

Children benefited significantly from their parents' increased availability, with improvements in the quality of family relations and indicators of child well-being. This suggests possibilities for breaking the intergenerational reproduction of alienated labor relations by modeling alternative approaches to time and leisure (Lareau, 2011). Nevertheless, the transformation of desire and the cultivation of genuinely playful practices depend on cultural infrastructures beyond working time reduction alone—public spaces for creative activity, community arts programs, and educational initiatives that develop capacities for non-instrumental enjoyment (Lefebvre, 1991a).

Spatial Reappropriation: The reduction in standard hours altered urban rhythms, potentially enabling more experimental uses of city life through changes in commuting patterns, modifications to peak-hour demand, and increased daytime activity in residential neighborhoods (Harvey, 2012). Some participants reported greater use of public spaces, increased walking and cycling, and more participation in local cultural and commercial offerings. These changes suggest possibilities for what Lefebvre (1991b) termed "spatial practice," which challenges the dominant urban organization based on work rhythms.

However, deep spatial transformation would require complementary investments in public space programming, cultural infrastructure, and transportation systems designed around multiple temporal rhythms rather than peak-hour commuting patterns. The persistence of car-dependent suburban sprawl and commercially oriented urban space limits the radical spatial implications of working time reduction without broader planning interventions (Brenner, 2009).

Détournement of Institutions: The Icelandic process demonstrated possibilities for institutional subversion, with unions and managers framing the reforms not as productivity-enhancing techniques but as fundamental revaluations of the role of work in life. The successful translation of the gains into collective bargaining suggests a move beyond isolated experiments toward a structural shift in the organization of work time (Frayne, 2019).

The policy represented what Debord (1967) termed *détournement*—the strategic appropriation and reorientation of existing institutions toward liberating ends. Unions, typically focused on wage improvements within capitalist frameworks, successfully championed a temporal liberation that challenges central assumptions about labor intensity and life organization (Brown, 2019). However, risks remain that working time reduction could be coopted and marketed as solely a productivity-enhancing tool, neutralizing the radical implications and integrating the reform back into capitalist efficiency narratives (Weeks, 2011).

4.1.4 Limitations and Context

Iceland's unique social and institutional context significantly limits the external generalizability of these results. High union density (over 90% of workers), coordinated collective bargaining systems, and a broad political consensus around social democratic values facilitated both the implementation and expansion processes, which may not be replicable elsewhere (Hayes, 2022). Iceland's small and relatively homogeneous population, along with strong social trust, enabled policy experimentation and learning that could face greater resistance in more diverse or polarized societies (Rothstein, 2005).

The country's economic structure also provided favorable conditions—high productivity levels, significant natural resource wealth, and strong export sectors that supported the fiscal capacity to maintain wages despite the reduction in hours. Lower-income countries with different economic structures might face greater tensions between working time reduction and economic development priorities (Rodriguez & Chen, 2021).

The voluntary nature of workplace participation also raises questions about selection effects—early adopters might have been better prepared to reorganize work processes, had stronger labor relations, or served populations more receptive to service changes, making them more likely to achieve positive outcomes (Berg et al., 2021). Organizations with more conflictual labor relations, rigid production processes, or external competitive pressures might experience different results.

Furthermore, the longer-term effects on cultural practices, ecological impacts, social solidarity, and macroeconomic performance require prolonged follow-up research. The four-year period, while longer than most working time reduction experiments, may be insufficient to capture deeper behavioral shifts, generational effects, or potential negative consequences that emerge over extended periods (New Economics Foundation, 2021; Antal et al., 2020). Economic recessions or external shocks could test the sustainability of working time reduction schemes when fiscal resources become constrained.

4.2 The Mondragón Cooperative Experience

Mondragón is often cited as one of the most significant experiments in cooperative ownership and democratic governance within a market economy. Founded in the Basque Country in the mid-twentieth century, the Mondragón Corporation has grown into a complex network of cooperatives operating across multiple sectors.

Mondragón is not treated here as representative of market socialism as a whole, but as a strategically chosen case through which to examine the tensions between democratic ownership, market coordination, and the reproduction of everyday social relations.

4.2.1 Historical Development

The Mondragón Cooperative Corporation (MCC), founded in the 1950s in the Spanish Basque Country, represents one of the world's largest and most extensively studied cooperative complexes. Emerging from a parish-level initiative led by the priest José María Arizmendiarrieta, Mondragón evolved from a small technical school and a single manufacturing cooperative into a federated network encompassing manufacturing, retail, finance, research, and education (Whyte & Whyte, 1991).

Arizmendiarrieta's vision combined Catholic social doctrine, Basque cultural nationalism, and a pragmatic strategy for economic development in post-Civil War Spain. Drawing on papal encyclicals that emphasized worker dignity and social solidarity, particularly *Rerum Novarum* (1891) and *Quadragesimo Anno* (1931), Arizmendiarrieta articulated a "humanistic concept of enterprise" that prioritized person-centered development over capital accumulation (Molina & MacLeod, 2020). This philosophical foundation resonated with Basque traditions of collective decisionmaking and mutual aid, providing cultural legitimacy for the cooperative experiments (Kasmir, 1996).

The institutional evolution unfolded in several phases. The initial phase (1956–1965) focused on establishing manufacturing cooperatives in metalworking and machine tools, building the technical school (later Mondragón University), and developing core cooperative principles (Azkarraga et al., 2012). The expansion phase (1965–1985) saw rapid growth in the number of cooperatives, the creation of Caja Laboral (the cooperative bank), and diversification into consumer goods, construction, and retail. The consolidation phase (1985–2008) involved federation into the unified MCC structure, international expansion, and the adoption of corporate management practices to compete in global markets.

The MCC's institutional architecture combines several innovative elements that address traditional cooperative challenges: worker ownership with democratic governance (one person, one vote), solidarity mechanisms for sharing risks and resources across cooperatives, a cooperative bank that provides patient capital and technical assistance, research and development institutions that foster innovation, and educational institutions that ensure skill formation and the cultural reproduction of cooperative values (Cheney, 1999). These features resonate with broader debates on "real utopias" as practical institutional alternatives that operate within capitalist frameworks (Wright, 2010a).

At its peak in the 2000s, Mondragón comprised over 250 cooperatives and subsidiary companies employing more than 100,000 worker-members and conventional employees, becoming Spain's fourth-largest business group by revenue and one of the world's largest cooperative networks (McCarthy et al., 2019). The system has demonstrated remarkable resilience, surviving economic crises such as the industrial restructuring of the 1970s, the 1993 Spanish recession, and the 2008–2012 European financial crisis while maintaining its cooperative principles and democratic governance structures.

4.2.2 *Institutional Innovations*

Mondragón's success is due in part to institutional innovations that address typical cooperative problems identified in the literature on collective action and workplace democracy (Hansmann, 1996; Craig, 1993). The cooperative bank (originally Caja Laboral, now Laboral Kutxa) provides patient capital, technical assistance, and business planning services, overcoming the traditional difficulty of cooperatives in accessing funding from conventional banks that are skeptical of democratic governance (Bretos et al., 2019).

Lending criteria based on a "social rate of return" evaluate projects based on job creation, regional development, and adherence to cooperative principles alongside financial profitability. This approach allows for long-term investments in research, development, and worker training that conventional capital markets often undervalue (Birchall & Hammond Ketilson, 2013). The bank also provides comprehensive business support through feasibility studies, market analysis, and management training, addressing coordination problems that plague isolated cooperatives.

Inter-cooperative solidarity mechanisms allow for risk-sharing and labor mobility within the network, providing a security that individual cooperatives could not achieve alone. The "solidarity fund" redistributes profits from successful cooperatives to support those facing difficulties, while labor mobility agreements allow for transferring workers between cooperatives during downturns rather than facing unemployment (Bretos et al., 2019). These mechanisms generate what economists term "risk-pooling" benefits while maintaining democratic governance at the firm level.

The educational institutions, including Mondragón University (founded in 1997), technical training centers, and continuing education programs, ensure both the development of technical skills and the cultural transmission of cooperative values across generations. This integration of education, research, and production represents a distinctive approach to knowledge creation and human development that challenges conventional separations between learning and working (Azkarraga et al., 2012). The university functions as a cooperative itself, with representation from faculty, staff, and students in governance, embedding democratic practices throughout the knowledge production process.

Governance structures attempt to balance democratic participation with operational efficiency through what Rothschild-Whitt (1979) terms "democratic bureaucracy." While workers elect management and define basic policies through General Assemblies and Social Councils, day-to-day operations are delegated to professional managers chosen for their technical competence (Heras-Saizarbitoria, 2016). This dual structure addresses tensions between participatory democracy and complex organizational coordination by creating differentiated spheres for strategic and operational decision-making.

Wage ratios are capped by democratic decisions, with historical commitments that top managers earn no more than six times the entry-level wage (compared to ratios of over 300:1 in large corporations). This "solidarity wage" system reflects cooperative values while providing sufficient incentives for managerial responsibility (Arando et al., 2015). However, these ratios have widened over time due to competitive pressures and difficulties in retaining top management.

Innovation systems integrate research and development across the network through shared facilities, collaborative projects, and technology transfer mechanisms. The network operates multiple R&D centers, maintains university partnerships, and invests approximately 5% of revenue in innovation activities—substantially more than typical Spanish manufacturing firms (Azkarraga et al., 2012). This collective approach to innovation allows smaller cooperatives to access advanced technologies and compete with large multinational corporations.

4.2.3 Challenges and Contradictions

Despite its achievements, Mondragón has faced significant tensions that illuminate broader contradictions between cooperative principles and the demands of the capitalist market. Pressures from globalization have forced difficult choices about international expansion, which led to the hiring of non-member workers in overseas plants who lack the voting rights, profit-sharing benefits, or job protections available to Basque cooperative members (Errasti et al., 2013).

This dual structure creates what critics term "cooperative imperialism"—the exploitation of conventional wage labor to sustain the cooperative benefits of core members (Kasmir, 1996). By 2010, nearly 40% of MCC employees worked in subsidiary firms without cooperative membership, which contradicts the core principles of universal membership and democratic participation. This development reflects broader challenges faced by worker cooperatives in competitive global markets, where labor cost advantages often determine survival (González & Marcuello, 2020).

The 2013 collapse of Fagor Electrodomésticos, Mondragón's flagship appliance manufacturer and its second-largest cooperative, exposed vulnerabilities in the solidarity system and raised questions about the effectiveness of democratic governance. Despite inter-cooperative support mechanisms valued at over 200 million euros, market pressures from Asian competition, strategic management errors, and the 2008 recession led to the bankruptcy that affected 5600 worker-members (Bretos et al., 2018).

The Fagor crisis revealed tensions between short-term market pressures and long-term cooperative development. Democratic decision-making processes proved slow to respond to rapidly changing competitive conditions, while solidarity mechanisms, though extensive, were insufficient to overcome fundamental problems of market position (Bakaikoa et al., 2017). The crisis forced difficult questions about the limits of cooperative solidarity in the face of structural economic changes beyond the control of the individual network.

Competitive pressures have also led to organizational changes that some critics interpret as "degeneration"—the gradual adoption of conventional corporate practices that undermine cooperative principles (Michels, 1915). This includes a reduction in worker participation in decision-making as operations become more complex, an increasing emphasis on efficiency and profitability over social goals, the adoption of performance management systems similar to conventional corporations, and the hiring of external professional managers without cooperative training or commitment (Kasmir, 1996).

The network has started to resemble what Boltanski and Chiapello (2005) terms "network capitalism"—flexible, project-based organizations that maintain cooperative legal forms while adopting market-oriented practices. This evolution raises fundamental questions about whether cooperative principles can survive intact in competitive market environments or whether they inevitably face pressures toward organizational isomorphism with conventional capitalist firms (DiMaggio & Powell, 1983).

Generational shifts present additional challenges, as younger worker-members, socialized into an increasingly individualistic and consumption-oriented culture, show less commitment to collective solidarity and democratic participation (Arrieta et al., 2018). Surveys indicate a decline in attendance at General Assemblies, less interest in cooperative education, and more individualistic career orientations among youth, which threatens the cultural reproduction essential for long-term cooperative sustainability.

4.2.4 *Situationist Analysis*

Spectacle and Alienation: Mondragón's worker ownership and democratic governance structures partially challenge the logic of the spectacle by integrating workers into production decisions and strategic planning processes. Greater job satisfaction, stronger identification with the work community, and an increased sense of agency among cooperative members suggest a reduction in alienation compared to conventional work relations (Arando et al., 2015). The elimination of traditional divisions between capital and labor creates possibilities for more authentic work relationships based on mutual cooperation rather than hierarchical control.

However, the network operates within competitive markets that require commodity production for exchange rather than use value, so the reproduction of the spectacle continues at macroeconomic levels. Cooperative firms must still compete for market share, maximize efficiency, and generate profits for reinvestment, creating pressures that can override democratic decision-making when survival is at stake (Lebowitz, 2012). Integration into global supply chains and consumer markets means that cooperative production ultimately serves the same spectacle of infinite accumulation that the Situationists critiqued.

Decommodification and Autonomy: Cooperative ownership provides greater job security, income stability, and voice in the workplace compared to conventional employment, representing a partial decommodification of the labor force. The democratic governance systems, profit-sharing arrangements, and collective ownership create forms of economic agency that are non-existent for typical wage laborers (Basterretxea and Albizu, 2019). Worker-members exert genuine influence over working conditions, investment priorities, and strategic direction through institutional channels.

The solidarity mechanisms also offer decommodified social protection through risk-sharing, labor mobility, and collective support in times of economic difficulty. These arrangements reduce individual dependence on market outcomes while maintaining productive activity, suggesting possibilities for what Gorz (1999) termed "liberated time" within work itself. Nevertheless, members remain fundamentally dependent on wages from the cooperative firms, and market pressures often force difficult decisions that limit democracy, particularly during economic crises when survival imperatives override participatory processes.

Everyday Life and Play: Mondragón's community orientation and solidarity practices foster more collective social relations than typical capitalist firms, creating supportive environments for member development that transcend the boundaries of the workplace. The educational opportunities, social services, cultural activities, and community investment programs create what Lefebvre (1991a) termed "social space" for authentic human development (Smith et al., 2020).

The integration of education, work, and community life through institutions like Mondragón University represents attempts to overcome the fragmentation of experience characteristic of capitalist social organization. Cooperative members report stronger community bonds, more meaningful work experiences, and greater coherence between personal values and everyday activities compared to conventional employees. However, the intensity of industrial work, competitive pressures, and efficiency requirements limit the possibilities for a creative and playful everyday life as imagined by the Situationist International, particularly in manufacturing cooperatives facing global competition.

Spatial Reappropriation: The network's regional focus has significantly reconfigured the Basque spatial economy by concentrating employment, community investment, educational infrastructure development, and local supplier relations. This territorial embeddedness represents a significant spatial reappropriation, where communities exercise democratic agency over economic development priorities rather than accepting externally imposed investment decisions (Greenwood & González Santos, 2019).

Mondragón's influence extends beyond direct employment to shape regional development patterns, support local small business networks, and maintain population in rural areas that might otherwise face depopulation. The integration of educational, financial, and productive activities creates what economic geographers term "local innovation systems" that strengthen regional resilience and self-determination (Morgan, 2004).

Nevertheless, globalization pressures have forced the relocation of production abroad, undermining localized control and creating spatial contradictions between cooperative principles and competitive requirements. The establishment of conventional subsidiaries in developing countries represents a form of spatial exploitation that contradicts the territorial solidarity that originally characterized the Mondragón model (Errasti et al., 2013).

Détournement of Institutions: Mondragón represents a large-scale institutional détournement, strategically reappropriating capitalist instruments—corporations, markets, banks, universities—for cooperative and community development rather than private capital accumulation. The cooperative bank exemplifies how financial institutions can be redirected toward solidarity lending and patient capital provision rather than profit maximization, while maintaining technical efficiency and financial sustainability (Clark & Mikami, 2019).

The university integration demonstrates a détournement of educational institutions, orienting knowledge production toward cooperative development and democratic skill formation rather than serving conventional corporate recruitment needs. This institutional reorientation suggests possibilities for broader social transformation through the strategic appropriation of existing structures rather than their total destruction.

However, pressures of scaling and exposure to the global market have induced the adoption of conventional corporate practices that reflect the logics Mondragón originally sought to transform. The hiring of non-member workers, the adoption of hierarchical management systems, and the emphasis on financial performance metrics represent processes of counter-détournement that neutralize the radical institutional innovations. Mondragón's institutional détournement remains, therefore, partial and contested, demonstrating both the possibilities and the limitations of working within market structures while attempting to transform their social logic.

4.2.5 *Lessons and Implications*

The Mondragón experience offers several insights for understanding the cooperative potential as a "non-reformist reform" that prefigures broader social transformation while addressing immediate needs. First, institutional innovation can create durable alternatives to conventional capitalist firms when it is backed by complementary institutions that address the traditional weaknesses of cooperativism: patient capital provision, risk-sharing mechanisms, technical assistance, educational systems, and cultural frameworks that sustain cooperative values across generations and economic cycles (Restakis, 2010).

Second, cooperatives face inherent tensions between the demands of democratic governance and the demands of market competitiveness that cannot be resolved through organizational design alone. External regulatory frameworks—cooperative-friendly regulations, public procurement preferences, patient capital provision, and protection from unfair competition—are necessary to create enabling environments for cooperative development and scaling (Wright, 2010a). Mondragón's relative success reflects a supportive regional and national context that may not be present elsewhere.

Third, the territorial embeddedness of cooperative networks can transform regional economies and spatial relations in ways that strengthen democratic control and community resilience. However, globalization pressures threaten this localized control by forcing cooperatives to compete internationally and establish conventional subsidiaries in low-wage regions. Maintaining cooperative principles while achieving scale remains an ongoing challenge that individual cooperative networks cannot address independently without broader international cooperation and solidarity.

Fourth, cultural reproduction is as crucial as economic performance for long-term cooperative sustainability. Educational institutions, social activities, and intergenerational value transmission systems require continuous investment and renewal to maintain commitment to democratic participation and collective solidarity, especially in increasingly individualistic and market-oriented cultural contexts (Baker, 2018).

From a Situationist perspective, Mondragón demonstrates that it is possible to establish alternative economic relations based on cooperation and democratic participation within capitalist structures, creating spaces for prefigurative politics and institutional experimentation. However, its transformative potential depends on broader cultural and political shifts that challenge the fundamental logic of capital accumulation and commodity production. Cooperatives can function as "laboratories" for democratic economic practices and as spaces of resistance to capitalist alienation, but they cannot, on their own, overcome the spectacle or achieve the revolution of everyday life that the Situationist International envisioned without complementary social movements and deeper political transformation.

4.3 Comparative Analysis

4.3.1 Divergent Trajectories Toward Social Transformation

The cases of Iceland and Mondragón reveal fundamentally different trajectories of institutional reform for advancing aspects of the Situationist project, each addressing distinct dimensions of capitalist alienation while facing particular limitations and possibilities. Iceland's working time reduction operates primarily through what Esping-Andersen (1990) terms temporal decommodification: lessening market control over time allocation, expanding individual autonomy, and creating material conditions for alternative life practices. This approach challenges what Thompson (1967) identified as the "temporal discipline" of industrial capitalism, with the potential to free up discretionary time for the construction of authentic experiences outside of market relations (Weeks, 2011).

The Mondragón cooperative model focuses on the democratization of ownership and collective solidarity, fundamentally transforming workplace relations and regional economic structures through what Wright (2010a) characterizes as "symbiotic transformation"—the building of alternative institutions within capitalist frameworks that demonstrate superior social outcomes. This approach addresses alienation at the point of production by eliminating the capital-labor divide and creating democratic governance structures that enable worker agency in economic decision-making (Lebowitz, 2012).

The temporal emphasis of the Icelandic reforms contrasts with Mondragón's focus on ownership and governance, suggesting different theoretical understandings of the primary sources of capitalist alienation. The Icelandic approach reflects post-Marxist theories that highlight the colonization of the lifeworld by system imperatives, where liberation requires defending temporal and spatial autonomy from market logic (Habermas, 1987). The Mondragón model aligns more closely with traditional Marxist analyses that prioritize democratic control over production processes as the basis for broader social transformation (Mies & Bennholdt-Thomsen, 1997).

From a Situationist perspective, both approaches address aspects of the spectacle's reproduction, though through different mechanisms. Working time reduction challenges the temporal organization that subordinates lived experience to the abstract time of labor, while cooperative ownership transforms the social relations through which commodities are produced. However, neither directly confronts what Debord (1967) identified as the cultural and psychological dimensions of the spectacle: the colonization of desire by commodity fetishism and passive consumption (Plant, 1992).

4.3.2 *Institutional Ecology and Support Networks*

Both cases demonstrate the crucial importance of institutional networks and supportive contexts for enabling and sustaining alternative economic arrangements. Iceland's success depended on coordinated labor relations systems, a consensual political culture, and high levels of social trust that facilitated both policy experimentation and rapid scaling through collective bargaining mechanisms (Rothstein, 2005). The country's corporatist institutions allowed unions, employers, and government to collaborate on policy learning rather than engaging in zero-sum conflicts over the organization of work time (Berg et al., 2021).

Iceland's broader cultural context was also crucial, including strong gender equality norms that legitimized work-life balance reforms, environmental awareness that supported reduced consumption patterns, and social democratic values that prioritize collective well-being alongside economic efficiency (Esping-Andersen, 1990). These cultural foundations provided normative support for reforms that might face greater resistance in more individualistic or market-fundamentalist societies (Hall & Soskice, 2001).

Mondragón's resilience and growth despite intense market pressures depended on its federated structure and complementary institutions that address traditional cooperative problems. The cooperative bank provides patient capital and technical assistance, overcoming market failures in financing democratic enterprises (Hansmann, 1996). The educational institutions ensure skill development and cultural reproduction, addressing human capital needs while transmitting cooperative values across generations (Azkarraga et al., 2012). The solidarity mechanisms allow for risk-sharing and mutual support, creating collective resilience that individual cooperatives could not achieve on their own (Bretos et al., 2019).

The territorial embeddedness of Mondragón's institutional network was also essential, generating what economic sociologists term "social capital" through dense relationships between cooperatives, suppliers, educational institutions, and local governments (Putnam, 2000). This territorial integration facilitates collective learning, technological exchange, and political influence that strengthen the entire cooperative ecosystem (Greenwood & González Santos, 2019).

Both cases illustrate what Polanyi (2001a) called the dynamics of the "double movement": market expansion generates social protective counter-movements, but requires institutional channels that translate social needs into effective political action. The Icelandic labor movement and the Mondragón cooperative federation provided such channels, demonstrating the necessity of organized collective action to sustain alternative economic arrangements in the face of market pressures and political opposition (Wright, 2019).

4.3.3 Risks of Cooptation and Structural Limitations

Nevertheless, both cases also illustrate significant risks of cooptation and structural limitations that constrain their transformative potential. The working time reduction reforms in Iceland face constant pressure to be reinterpreted as productivity-enhancing techniques in the service of capital accumulation, rather than as a challenge to the centrality of work in social organization (Weeks, 2011). The management literature is increasingly promoting "work-life balance" as a human resources strategy to improve job performance and reduce turnover costs, potentially neutralizing the radical implications of temporal liberation (Brown, 2019).

The integration of this policy into collective bargaining systems, while enabling its expansion, also risks institutionalizing it, stripping away its experimental and transformative elements. As working time reduction becomes normalized within existing labor relations, it may lose its capacity to inspire broader questioning of the social role of work and the possibility of a more fundamental economic reorganization (Frayne, 2019). The reform's success within capitalist frameworks could, paradoxically, strengthen the system's legitimacy by addressing worker grievances without challenging the underlying power structures.

The Mondragón cooperatives have faced similar cooptation pressures, adopting competitive behaviors and management practices that reproduce capitalist logics under collective ownership forms. The hiring of non-member workers in subsidiary operations, the adoption of performance management systems resembling conventional corporations, and the emphasis on financial metrics over social goals represent what Michels (1915) termed "oligarchical" tendencies—the gradual transformation of democratic organizations into bureaucratic hierarchies serving elite interests (Kasmir, 1996).

The network's integration into global supply chains and capital markets creates structural pressures that can override democratic decision-making when survival is at stake. The Fagor crisis demonstrated how market imperatives can force cooperatives to abandon principles of solidarity and adopt conventional business practices, suggesting limits to democratic control in competitive capitalist environments (González & Marcuello, 2020). These developments reflect broader theoretical debates about whether alternative economic forms can maintain their distinctive character while achieving the necessary scale and efficiency within capitalist markets (Gibson-Graham, 2006a).

Both cases also face what Boltanski and Chiapello (2005) term "recuperation" by the "new spirit of capitalism"—the system's ability to incorporate critique and transform it into sources of renewed accumulation. Working time reduction becomes "flexible work arrangements" that increase productivity, while cooperative enterprises become models of "stakeholder capitalism" that legitimize market relations through participatory rhetoric (Chiapello, 2007). This recuperation process suggests that institutional reforms alone are insufficient to challenge the fundamental logic of capitalism without complementary cultural and political transformation.

4.3.4 *Criteria for Situationist-Aligned Reforms*

The comparative analysis suggests that reforms most aligned with Situationist goals are those that systematically address multiple dimensions of capitalist alienation while building capacity for broader social transformation. Specifically, transformative reforms should:

(1) **Reduce dependence on wage labor and market imperatives** by providing decommodification mechanisms that offer economic security independent of market outcomes. Maintained wages during reduced hours in Iceland and collective ownership in Mondragón partially achieve this by reducing individual vulnerability to market fluctuations. However, more radical decommodification would require universal basic services, access to commons, or post-monetary economic relations that completely eliminate wage dependence (Gorz, 1999).

(2) **Expand time and space for non-commodified activities** by creating material conditions for authentic experiences outside of market relations. The temporal liberation in Iceland and community investment in Mondragón generate opportunities for creative, social, and political activities that resist commodification. Yet, realizing this potential requires complementary cultural infrastructure: public spaces, artistic resources, educational opportunities, and social movements that cultivate capacities for non-instrumental enjoyment and collective creativity (Lefebvre, 1991a).

(3) **Foster democratic participation and collective decision-making** beyond formal political institutions, including in the organization of economic and social life. Workplace democracy in Mondragón and participatory policy experimentation in Iceland demonstrate possibilities for extending democratic principles into previously authoritarian domains. However, genuine democratization requires addressing power inequalities based on class, gender, race, and other hierarchies that limit meaningful participation (Young, 2000).

(4) **Challenge dominant cultural values on work, consumption, and success** by demonstrating alternative bases for social recognition and personal fulfillment. Both cases offer models of life organization that prioritize well-being, solidarity, and community over individual wealth accumulation and consumption. Nevertheless, cultural

transformation requires sustained ideological work, educational initiatives, and media representations that legitimize alternative value systems (Gramsci, 1971).

(5) **Create solidarity networks that can resist competitive pressures and political backlash** through mutual support mechanisms that enable collective resilience. Inter-cooperative solidarity in Mondragón and union coordination in Iceland demonstrate how institutional networks can protect alternative arrangements from market and political pressures. However, broader transformation requires international solidarity networks capable of coordinating resistance to global capital and supporting alternative development models (Santos, 2006).

4.3.5 *Prefigurative Politics and Movement Building*

Neither case achieves the comprehensive transformation of everyday life advocated by the Situationist International, but both create material and cultural conditions that could sustain more radical experimentation in what social movement theorists call "prefigurative politics"—the embodiment of desired social changes within contemporary struggles (Breines, 1982). Prefigurative practices demonstrate alternative possibilities while building capacity for broader transformation through skill development, consciousness-raising, and relationship building (Yates, 2015).

The Icelandic working time experiments function as prefigurative politics by demonstrating that an alternative temporal organization is possible, while building political bases for a broader labor market transformation. The policy's success challenges dominant assumptions about the productivity-hours relationship and the necessity of work for social organization, potentially inspiring a wider questioning of capitalist labor regimes (Weeks, 2011). The participatory evaluation process also develops democratic capacity and policy learning skills that could underpin more ambitious institutional experiments.

The Mondragón cooperative network represents a more comprehensive prefigurative politics by creating alternative economic relations that show superior social outcomes compared to conventional capitalist firms. The network's educational, financial, and productive institutions provide concrete models of post-capitalist economic organization, while developing technical skills, democratic practices, and solidarity relations necessary for broader transformation (Wright, 2010a). The cooperative's success challenges neoliberal claims about market efficiency and the incompatibility with democratic governance.

However, both cases also illustrate the limitations of prefigurative politics when it is isolated from broader social movements and structural change. The Icelandic reforms remain constrained by capitalist labor relations and could be reversed in the face of future political shifts or economic crises. The Mondragón cooperatives face constant pressure to adopt conventional business practices and have been unable to prevent broader trends of neoliberalization in Spanish society (Harvey, 2005).

4.3.6 Movement Catalyzing Potential

The Situationist potential of both cases ultimately depends on whether they inspire and enable broader social movements that challenge the underlying structures of the spectacle, rather than merely generating better conditions within existing arrangements. This catalyzing function requires several conditions that neither case has fully achieved.

First, institutional experiments must be connected to broader social movements that can articulate links between specific reforms and comprehensive social transformation. The working time reduction in Iceland grew out of labor movement activism but has not generated broader movements that question capitalism's growth imperatives or commodity relations. Mondragón's cooperative development has inspired similar initiatives globally, but it remains disconnected from anticapitalist movements that challenge private ownership or market logic (Gibson-Graham, 2006a).

Second, reforms must be framed in ways that reveal, rather than conceal, underlying power relations and structural limitations. Both cases risk being interpreted as proof that capitalism can be humanized through minor reforms, rather than as evidence that alternative economic relations are possible and necessary. This approach requires what Freire (2000) termed "critical consciousness"—analytical frameworks that connect personal experiences with systemic structures and possibilities for transformation.

Third, successful experiments must be scaled and replicated in ways that maintain their transformative potential, rather than being coopted by existing institutions. The success of collective bargaining in Iceland and Mondragón's replication attempts demonstrate possibilities for scaling, but also risks of institutionalization that strip away experimental elements.

Scaling transformative reforms requires what Santos (2006) terms "translation work"—adapting successful practices to different contexts while maintaining core principles and radical vision.

Fourth, institutional experiments must build capacity for broader political action, rather than creating isolated alternatives that accommodate themselves to existing power structures. The success of the Icelandic policy and Mondragón's economic achievements could reduce incentives for broader political engagement by improving conditions for certain populations, leaving fundamental structures intact. Avoiding this "reformist trap" requires connecting specific improvements with broader movements for systemic change (Gorz, 1967).

The comparative analysis thus reveals both the potential and the limitations of institutional reform as a Situationist strategy. While neither case achieves the comprehensive transformation of everyday life that the SI advocated, both demonstrate that alternative economic relations are possible and can deliver superior social outcomes under specific conditions. Their revolutionary potential depends on whether they inspire broader movements that challenge the fundamental structures of capitalism, rather than merely improving conditions within existing arrangements. This requires sustained political work that connects immediate reforms with a vision of long-term transformation, while building collective capacity for more radical experimentations.

CHAPTER 5

Criticisms, Limitations, and Responses

The central argument of this study—that social-democratic and market socialist reforms can serve as pathways toward a post-spectacular society—faces several significant criticisms that must be addressed directly. Rather than treating these as external obstacles, this chapter recognizes them as constitutive tensions within the analytical framework itself. The approach here is twofold: first, to present each criticism in its strongest form; second, to develop responses that clarify the scope, ambitions, and limitations of the book's central claims. Four interconnected areas of concern structure this discussion: the risk of cooptation and reproduction of the spectacle, questions of generalizability across contexts, challenges of theoretical translation, and temporal-structural constraints on institutional change.

5.1 Cooptation and the Reproduction of the Spectacle

5.1.1 *The Orthodox Situationist Critique*

The most fundamental critique, particularly from a purist Situationist perspective, holds that any institutional reform, regardless of its emancipatory intent, ultimately becomes coopted by the very spectacle it seeks to subvert. This argument, grounded in Debord (1967)'s analysis of spectacular

M. Brum, *Democratic Alternatives*,
https://doi.org/10.1007/978-3-032-23153-6_5

capitalism's totalizing logic, maintains that capitalist institutions are inherently designed to assimilate and neutralize radical impulses by transforming them into marketable commodities, bureaucratic procedures, or efficiency-enhancing mechanisms (Jappe, 1999).

Contemporary critical theorists have extended this argument considerably. Boltanski and Chiapello (2005) document how critiques of bureaucratic alienation from the 1960s were recuperated into "network capitalism," which emphasizes flexibility, autonomy, and creativity while maintaining fundamental power structures. Similarly, Chiapello (2007) analyzes how artistic and social critiques of capitalism become integrated into management discourse and organizational practices, ultimately serving capital accumulation rather than challenging it.

From this theoretical perspective, working time reduction policies risk reinterpretation as human resources management techniques that improve worker productivity and reduce turnover costs, thus serving capital's interests rather than questioning work's centrality in social organization (Weeks, 2011). The abundant management literature promoting "work-life balance" as a competitive advantage suggests this recuperation is already occurring, with corporations adopting flexible arrangements to enhance employee performance rather than challenging fundamental assumptions about the wage-labor relationship (Brown, 2019).

Cooperative enterprises face similar pressures to adopt conventional business practices as they scale and compete in capitalist markets. Kasmir (1996) argues that Mondragón's evolution demonstrates the inevitable "degeneration" of cooperative principles under market pressures, while McCarthy et al. (2019) document parallel patterns in diverse cooperative movements where democratic governance yields to managerial efficiency and social goals become subordinated to financial performance.

The recuperation thesis suggests that spectacular capitalism possesses sophisticated mechanisms for neutralizing opposition by incorporating it into system-maintaining functions. Marcuse (1969) theorized this as "repressive tolerance"—the system's ability to tolerate and even celebrate dissent while preventing it from achieving transformative effects. Contemporary media and consumer culture demonstrate a remarkable capacity to commodify rebellion, transforming revolutionary symbols, practices, and ideas into lifestyle choices and market niches (Heath & Potter, 2004).

5.1.2 Response: Contingency, Struggle, and Strategic Framing

This critique is both valid and indispensable—it prevents naive optimism about institutional transformation. Yet rather than invalidating reformist experimentation, it should serve as a strategic compass. The response developed here is dialectical, recognizing both risks and possibilities within institutional change processes.

First, cooptation is not an inevitable outcome but a constant risk requiring active political struggle to prevent neutralization of transformative potential. The emancipatory potential of any reform depends heavily on its design, implementation process, funding mechanisms, cultural framing, and ongoing political mobilization surrounding it (Wright, 2019).

The Icelandic case demonstrates possibilities for successful *détournement* of institutional frameworks when unions and civil society organizations frame reforms to challenge rather than reinforce capitalist logic. Unions presented working time reduction not as a productivity boost but as fundamental reevaluation of work's role in human life, connecting temporal liberation to broader issues of gender equality, environmental sustainability, and democratic participation (Berg et al., 2021). The successful translation of pilot experiments into collective bargaining achievements covering 85% of the workforce suggests institutional reforms can become terrain where spectacular logic is actively contested from within existing structures.

The concept of "non-reformist reforms," developed by Gorz (1967) and refined by theorists like Wright (2010a), provides frameworks for distinguishing between reforms strengthening existing power structures and those building capacity for broader transformation. Non-reformist reforms characteristically: (1) improve immediate conditions while revealing structural constraints; (2) build collective capacity for future struggles; (3) shift power relations favoring dominated groups; (4) challenge dominant ideological frameworks; and (5) create institutional spaces for democratic experimentation (Löwy, 2018).

The Mondragón cooperative network demonstrates such non-reformist characteristics by creating alternative economic relations challenging private ownership and workplace hierarchy while developing technical skills, democratic practices, and solidarity relations necessary for broader economic transformation. Despite facing market pressures and organizational challenges, the network continues providing models for post-capitalist economic organization and inspiring cooperative development globally (Restakis, 2010).

Second, we reject binary frameworks pitting "pure revolution" against "total spectacle," instead adopting what Benjamin (1968b) termed "dialectical images"—approaches recognizing contradictory tendencies within social phenomena. The Situationist framework itself contains resources for non-binary analysis, particularly in Vaneigem (2012)'s emphasis on everyday life transformation and Lefebvre's (Lefebvre, 1991a) analysis of spatial contradictions creating resistance possibilities within dominant structures.

Our analytical categories—spectacle and alienation, decommodification and autonomy, everyday life and play, spatial reappropriation, and institutional *détournement*—are designed precisely to measure degrees of emancipation rather than assuming binary outcomes. This methodological approach allows evaluating whether specific reforms advance or restrict possibilities for authentic experience, democratic participation, and collective solidarity (Holloway, 2002).

5.1.3 Strategic Considerations for Preventing Cooptation

Based on historical analysis of social movement outcomes, several strategic considerations can reduce cooptation risks and enhance institutional reforms' transformative potential.

First, reforms must integrate within broader social movements maintaining pressure for ongoing transformation rather than accepting limited gains as sufficient. The civil rights movement's combination of institutional legal strategies with grass-roots mobilization illustrates how reform campaigns can maintain transformative momentum when connecting with broader social justice struggles (McAdam, 1999). Iceland's working time reduction succeeded partly because it remained connected to labor movement activism for broader workplace democracy and gender equality rather than becoming an isolated policy experiment.

Second, successful reforms require what Gramsci (1971) termed "counter-hegemonic" cultural work challenging dominant ideological frameworks while building alternative common sense. This involves reconfiguring problems to reveal structural constraints and connect ndividual experiences with collective change possibilities. Environmental movements' success establishing climate change as systemic rather than individual demonstrates how cultural work prevents cooptation by maintaining focus on structural transformation rather than behavioral modification (Klein, 2014).

Third, reforms must build institutional capacity for democratic participation instead of relying solely on elite policymaking or technocratic implementation. Participatory budgeting experiments in Brazil and elsewhere demonstrate how institutional innovations can strengthen rather than weaken grassroots political capacity when designed to complement rather than substitute popular mobilization (Baiocchi, 2005). Mondragón's educational institutions serve similar functions by developing both technical skills and democratic practices necessary for cooperative governance.

Fourth, transformative reforms require international solidarity networks resist ing capital mobility and political pressure from dominant classes. The European cooperative movement's development through transnational support networks and policy coordination mechanisms illustrates how local experiments can be protected and scaled through international organizing (Birchall & Hammond Ketilson, 2013). Climate justice movements' emphasis on "just transition" policies demonstrates how reform demands can be framed to build international solidarity while addressing immediate needs (Stevis & Felli, 2018).

5.2 Generalizability and Contextual Specificity

5.2.1 The Challenge of Context-Dependence

A major critique concerns our empirical findings' generalizability to different social, cultural, and political contexts. Both Icelandic and Mondragón cases are nested in unique institutional, cultural, and economic configurations that may not be easily replicable elsewhere, raising questions about whether observed outcomes can be achieved under different conditions (Flyvbjerg, 2006).

Iceland's working time reduction experiment succeeded within distinctive institutional contexts characterized by exceptionally high union density (over 90% of workers), coordinated collective bargaining systems covering most sectors, consensual political culture emphasizing compromise and experimentation, and high social trust and civic engagement levels (Berg et al., 2021). These enabling conditions reflect decades of social-democratic institution-building and cultural development generating favorable environments for political experimentation and rapid implementation through established labor relations mechanisms.

The country's economic structure also provided unusual advantages. Iceland's high productivity levels, significant natural resource wealth (particularly geothermal and hydropower), strong export sectors, and relatively small homogeneous population allowed wage maintenance despite work hour reductions while limiting complex coordination problems larger, more diverse economies might face (Rodriguez & Chen, 2021). The 2008 financial crisis and subsequent economic restructuring may have created additional openings for policy experimentation unavailable in more stable economic contexts.

Similarly, Mondragón's success reflects highly specific historical and cultural conditions potentially unreplicable elsewhere. The network emerged within Basque cultural contexts emphasizing collective decision-making, mutual aid, and resistance to external domination, providing cultural legitimacy for cooperative experimentation possibly absent in more individualistic societies (Kasmir, 1996). Catholic social doctrine's influence, particularly emphasis on human dignity and social solidarity, offered ideological resources for challenging capitalist work organization possibly less available in secular or Protestant contexts (Molina & MacLeod, 2020).

Post-Civil War Spanish contexts created unique cooperative development opportunities, including limited state economic development capacity, alternative job creation needs in peripheral regions, and political space for local economic experimentation within national authoritarian frameworks. Contemporary democratic contexts with greater state capacity and more integrated markets may offer fewer opportunities for autonomous cooperative development (Whyte & Whyte, 1991).

5.2.2 *Response: Scope Conditions and Principles of Adaptation*

While recognizing these contextual specificities, comparative case analysis can identify **scope conditions**—contexts within which similar outcomes could be reached—instead of requiring exact institutional arrangement replication. Our methodological approach draws on Ragin (2000) and Mahoney and Goertz (2012) frameworks for "configurational analysis," identifying condition combinations enabling certain out comes rather than seeking universal causal laws.

The goal is not to propose Icelandic or Mondragón cases as universal "templates" but as **illustrative laboratories**. They reveal enabling conditions, risks, and mechanisms informing context-specific strategies elsewhere. The analytical framework developed in Chapter 3—focused on decommodification, autonomy, everyday life, and spatial reappropriation—functions as **criteria**, not blueprints. The objective isn't replicating Mondragón everywhere but asking: under what conditions do cooperatives sustain democratic governance? When does working time reduction enhance autonomy rather than productivity?

Comparative analysis of working time reduction experiments across countries reveals several enabling conditions appearing necessary but not individually sufficient for successful implementation: strong labor organizing capacity, coordinated employer-union relations, favorable public policy frameworks, and cultural legitimacy for work-life balance priorities (Hayden, 2006). These conditions exist in diverse combinations across different contexts, suggesting adaptation possibilities rather than requiring identical institutional arrangements.

Belgian and French working time reduction experiments, though less comprehensive than Iceland's, show similar positive results under distinct institutional conditions, including more conflictual labor relations and greater employer resistance. The key difference appears to be supportive government policies and strong union mobilization capacity rather than consensual political culture (Cette et al., 2013a). This suggests Iceland's consensual approach represents one among several possible working time reduction pathways.

Rather than offering universal blueprints, our case studies identify **principles of adaptation** guiding similar initiatives in different contexts while respecting local conditions and constraints. These principles emerge from theoretical analysis of enabling conditions combined with practical implementation experience.

First, successful reforms require what social movement theorists call "political opportunity structures"—institutional channels, elite divisions, and cultural resources enabling collective action for change (Tarrow, 2011). Coordinated labor relations in Iceland and Mondragón's regional autonomy provided such opportunities, but similar structures could exist elsewhere in different forms—civil society organizational capacity, progressive local governments, supportive religious institutions, or international development funding.

Second, transformative reforms must build on existing cultural and institutional resources rather than attempting complete foreign model transplantation. Icelandic working time reduction succeeded by connecting with established gender equality and environmental awareness norms, while Mondragón drew on Basque collective traditions and Catholic social doctrine. Similar initiatives in other contexts should identify local cultural and institutional resources legitimizing and supporting alternative economic arrangements (Gibson-Graham, 2006a).

Third, successful scalability requires what Santos (2006) terms "translation work"—adapting successful practices to different contexts while maintaining essential principles and transformative vision. This involves identifying essential elements requiring preservation versus contextual features permitting modification. For working time reduction, essential elements include wage maintenance, democratic workplace decision-making, and connection to broader social movement goals, while specific hourly reductions, sectoral implementation, and policy mechanisms can vary considerably.

The generalizability limitation doesn't invalidate case study findings but emphasizes contextual adaptation importance guided by theoretical understanding of enabling conditions and transformative mechanisms. Our framework provides analytical tools evaluating potential reforms in specific contexts rather than prescriptive universally applicable models.

5.3 Theoretical Translation and Methodological Fidelity

5.3.1 *The Challenge of Conceptual Coherence*

A fundamental methodological critique questions whether it's intellectually valid translating a revolutionary anti-institutional critique like the Situationist International's into an analytical framework evaluating institutional reforms. Critics might argue SI concepts such as *dérive*, *détournement*, and spectacle constitute total rejection of formal politics and institutional engagement, making their reform evaluation use a theoretical contradiction diluting their radical content (Plant, 1992).

This critique reflects broader radical theory tensions between "revolutionary" and "reformist" social change approaches. Orthodox Situationist theory interpretations emphasize its rejection of all existing institution engagement forms, viewing any state power, electoral politics, or market relations interaction as inevitable cooptation (Jappe, 1999). From this perspective, institutional reforms cannot serve revolutionary ends because working within existing structures reinforces their legitimacy and channels radical energy into system-maintaining activities.

Contemporary radical theorists have extended similar arguments, suggesting institutional engagement creates "participatory traps" absorbing social movement energy while preventing more fundamental power structure challenges (Piven, 2006). Holloway (2002) advocates "changing the world without taking power" precisely to avoid such cooptation risks, while Day (2005) argues anarchist approaches emphasizing prefigurative politics and autonomous organizing offer more promising pathways than institutional engagement.

Theoretical translation challenges also involve conceptual coherence questions when applying concepts developed for one historical context (1960s French capitalism) to contemporary conditions (twenty-first-century globalized capitalism with different institutional arrangements and cultural contexts). Merrifield (2005) argues Debord's spectacle analysis requires substantial updating addressing contemporary developments in digital media, financialization, and global commodity chains transforming spectacular relations functioning.

5.3.2 Response: Methodological Innovation with Theoretical Fidelity

Our response to theoretical translation concerns emphasizes methodological innovation maintaining fidelity to Situationist insights while extending their analytical applicability to contemporary conditions. This is a serious concern requiring careful navigation. Yet concepts don't remain frozen in original formulations; they migrate, mutate, and acquire new meanings in different contexts.

We distinguish between using Situationist theory *as* political practice versus *as* analytical framework understanding social change possibilities. We don't claim institutional reform *is* Situationist praxis as advocated by Debord (1967) and Vaneigem (2012). Rather, we argue certain reforms can create *conditions of possibility* for authentic revolutionary praxis emerging by reducing spectacular integration, expanding temporal and spatial autonomy, and building collective self-organization capacity.

The wager isn't "domesticating" Situationism but **deploying its critique as a lens**. This implies retaining its hostility to representation, alienation, and commodification while acknowledging contemporary struggles must often operate within and against institutions (Holloway, 2002). Far from betraying Situationism, this use keeps alive its critical edge: by applying it to reforms, we illuminate their limits, neutralization risks, and experimentation openings.

This approach draws on Benjamin (1968b)'s "dialectical images" concept, identifying revolutionary potential within seemingly reformist phenomena without collapsing reform/revolution distinctions. Benjamin's analysis of nineteenth-century Parisian arcades as prefiguring both spectacular commodity display and revolutionary *flânerie* possibilities offers methodological guidance identifying contradictory tendencies within institutional arrangements (Buck-Morss, 1992).

Our analytical categories—spectacle and alienation, decommodification and autonomy, everyday life and play, spatial reappropriation, and institutional *détournement*—are designed precisely measuring whether reforms move away from or reinforce spectacular logics without assuming predetermined outcomes. This methodological approach allows evaluating transformation degrees rather than binary revolutionary/counter-revolutionary classifications often paralyzing radical analysis (Wright, 2019).

Moreover, contemporary capitalism—digitalized, globalized, ecologically unstable—presents alienation forms Debord and Vaneigem only anticipated. Translating their critique into this new context isn't dilution but renewal. Fidelity to theory requires adaptation, not dogmatic repetition (Srnicek, 2017; Zuboff, 2019).

The framework draws on Lefebvre (1991a)'s methodological innovations analyzing contradictory tendencies within everyday life under capitalism. Lefebvre showed how spatial and temporal arrangements simultaneously reproduce and potentially subvert capitalist social relations, offering methodological precedents for dialectical institutional reform analysis. His "differential space" concept offers tools understanding how alternative spatial practices can emerge within and against dominant spatial organization (Lefebvre, 1991b).

We employ multi-methodological approaches combining quantitative outcome measurement with ethnographic lived experience and cultural transformation analysis. This methodological pluralism seeks capturing both material effects (work hours, wages, productivity, health outcomes) and cultural dimensions (meaning, relations quality, political consciousness, collective capacity) that purely statistical or qualitative approaches might miss (Creswell & Creswell, 2017).

5.4 Temporal Dynamics and Structural Constraints

5.4.1 The Challenge of Long-Term Sustainability

A critical limitation concerns social change temporal dimensions and whether institutional reforms can maintain transformative potential over extended periods. Case studies examined here provide relatively short-term evidence (four-year Iceland experiment, Mondragón experience analyzed primarily over decades rather than generations), raising questions whether observed positive outcomes can be sustained and deepened over longer timeframes or inevitably face entropy, cooptation, or setbacks facing changing conditions.

Social democratic reforms historical analysis suggests complex temporal dynamics where initial transformative potential gradually erodes through institutionalization processes, elite capture, and political context shifts (Korpi, 2002). Swedish model evolution from 1970s through neoliberal restructuring demonstrates how even highly successful institutional innovations can be undermined by global economic pressures, demographic changes, and fluctuating political coalitions (Ryner, 2002). Mondragón's own evolution illustrates these temporal tensions, with cooperative principles under constant pressure from competitive market dynamics, generational changes, and globalization processes creating structural incentives for conventional business practices. Non-member worker hiring in subsidiary operations and hierarchical management system adoption suggest cooperative "degeneration" may be endemic rather than contingent, requiring continuous political work preventing it (Michels, 1915).

Even when reforms initially succeed, capitalism's structural dynamics tend eroding them over time. Cooperatives may degenerate, welfare states may retreat under fiscal pressures, and shorter workweeks may be reabsorbed into productivity-driven logics. From this view, reforms are temporary islands soon reintegrated into system reproduction (Offe, 1984; O'Connor, 1973).

Market competition generates systemic pressures toward efficiency maximization overriding democratic governance and social goals over time. Cooperative enterprises face constant pressure adopting conventional business practices when competing with capitalist firms externalizing social and environmental costs while concentrating decision-making authority (Bowles & Gintis, 2011). Even successful cooperatives may find maintaining market position requires compromising essential principles, leading to gradual transformation into conventional businesses with cooperative legal forms.

5.4.2 *Response: Building Durable Transformation Capacity*

This is undeniably true in many historical cases. Yet temporariness shouldn't be confused with futility. Reforms can open **experimentation spaces** altering collective capacities, imaginaries, and subjectivities—even if later constrained. Swedish welfare state, despite neoliberal retrenchment, permanently transformed citizenship expectations (Esping-Andersen, 1990). Mondragón, despite contradictions, has provided generations of workers with democratic self-management experiences continuing to inspire new cooperative movements (Kasmir, 1996).

The question isn't whether reforms can escape structural pressures indefinitely but whether they can **catalyze new struggle, consciousness, and organization forms**. If reforms are articulated with broader movements and sustained by collective agency, their transformative effects can endure beyond institutional rollback (Wright, 2010a).

These temporal and structural limitations suggest strategic implications for institutional reform approaches recognizing constraints while identifying sustained transformation possibilities. The analysis points to several considerations enhancing reform initiatives' long-term viability and transformative potential.

First, successful reforms must build cultural and educational infrastructure sustaining alternative values and practices across generational shifts and changing economic conditions. Mondragón's educational institutions and Iceland's participatory policy development processes demonstrate long-term capacity building importance rather than focusing solely on immediate political outcomes (Azkarraga et al., 2012).

Second, institutional reforms require protective mechanisms resisting cooptation pressures and maintaining transformative orientation over time. This may involve constitutional protections, international solidarity networks, or cultural/religious institutional embeddedness providing resources resisting market pressures and political backlash (Polanyi, 2001a).

Third, transformative reforms must connect to broader social movements exerting ongoing political pressure for sustained innovation and cooptation resistance. Isolated institutional experiments are more vulnerable to cooptation than those embedded within active political constituencies defending and expanding their transformative potential (Piven & Cloward, 2009).

Fourth, long-term transformation may require what Wright (2010a) terms "interstitial" and "symbiotic" strategies building alternative arrangements within existing structures while working toward broader structural change. This suggests institutional reforms should be evaluated not as ends in themselves but as components of long-term transformation strategies possibly requiring multiple generations achieving comprehensive change.

5.5 Strategic Synthesis and Way Forward

Taken together, these criticisms highlight that institutional reforms are not sufficient conditions for emancipation—but they may be **necessary conditions** for creating openings. The response is thus twofold:

1. To remain attentive to cooptation, degeneration, and erosion risks.
2. To design reforms as prefigurative, linked to social movements, and oriented toward autonomy rather than mere efficiency.

This dialectical stance neither fetishizes reforms nor dismisses them. It recognizes that in institutional experimentation interstices lie possibilities for Situationist-inspired transformations.

The criticisms reviewed—on cooptation, generalizability, conceptual fidelity, and structural constraints—are not obstacles to the argument but constitutive tensions. They sharpen the book's claims and clarify its scope: the point isn't proposing Situationist social democracy but using Situationism as critical compass evaluating reforms, identifying when they reinforce alienation and when they open cracks toward autonomy and creativity.

By engaging with these critiques, the book situates itself in ongoing debates between reform and revolution, theory and praxis, structure and agency. The hope isn't resolving this tension but keeping it alive—because in that unresolved space new collective imagination and emancipatory practice forms can emerge.

The temporal limitation doesn't invalidate institutional reform approaches but emphasizes strategic thinking importance about how specific reforms contribute to long-term transformation processes while maintaining awareness of structural constraints and cooptation risks. Our framework provides tools for such strategic evaluation rather than definitive reform potential judgments.

5.6 Conclusion

The criticisms reviewed—on cooptation, generalizability, conceptual fidelity, and structural constraints—are not obstacles to the argument but constitutive tensions. They sharpen the book's claims and clarify its scope: the point is not to propose a Situationist social democracy, but to use Situationism as a critical compass to evaluate reforms, to identify when they reinforce alienation and when they open cracks toward autonomy and creativity.

By engaging with these critiques, the book situates itself in an ongoing debate between reform and revolution, theory and praxis, structure and agency. The hope is not to resolve this tension, but to keep it alive—because it is in that unresolved space that new forms of collective imagination and emancipatory practice can emerge.

CHAPTER 6

Conclusion

The present study proposes an analytical framework that seeks to reconcile Situationist critique with the evaluation of institutional reforms, arguing that cooptation is not an inevitable outcome but a constant risk that must be managed through political action, critical reflection, and sustained social mobilization. The research maintains that the emancipatory potential of any reform depends on multiple interrelated factors: the structural design of the policy, the implementation mechanisms, available financial resources, how it is culturally framed and communicated, and the political and social mobilization that accompanies it over time.

The arguments developed in this book engage with a growing and increasingly diverse body of scholarship that has sought to rethink alternatives to capitalism in the context of recurrent economic crises, ecological breakdown, and processes of democratic erosion. Since the global financial crisis of 2008, and even more visibly in the aftermath of the COVID-19 pandemic, a renewed interest in systemic alternatives has emerged across political economy, geography, sociology, and political theory. This literature has reopened debates around ownership, coordination, and democratic control that were largely marginalized during the high point of neoliberal hegemony, when market allocation and shareholder value were treated as both analytically inevitable and normatively desirable. The contemporary moment is thus marked by what Fraser (2022) characterizes as a crisis of

M. Brum, *Democratic Alternatives*,
https://doi.org/10.1007/978-3-032-23153-6_6

hegemony—a juncture in which the legitimacy of capitalist institutions is contested even as viable alternatives remain contested and emergent.

A prominent strand of this renewed debate is associated with the Democracy Collaborative and the Next System Project, which advance a set of institutional strategies aimed at building post-capitalist trajectories through democratic ownership, anchor institutions, and place-based forms of economic organization (Speth & Courrier, 2016; Alperovitz, 2016). Rather than proposing a single blueprint for systemic change, these contributions emphasize cumulative and path-dependent processes of transformation, grounded in local institutions, municipal governance, and durable social coalitions. Their focus on experimentation, institutional layering, and the strategic use of existing public and quasi-public actors resonates strongly with this book's concern for moving beyond both market fundamentalism and statecentric models of centralized planning. Building on this work, Guinan and O'Neill (2019) elaborates a theory of "systemic economic democracy" that seeks to integrate diverse democratic ownership forms—cooperatives, community land trusts, municipal enterprises, and public banks—into coherent regional ecosystems capable of challenging capitalist hegemony at multiple scales simultaneously.

The institutional turn in post-capitalist thinking has also been enriched by engagement with historical experiences of economic transformation. Hanna (2018) examines how public ownership models evolved across different national contexts, demonstrating that state ownership need not replicate the bureaucratic pathologies associated with Soviet-style planning when embedded within democratic accountability structures and participatory governance mechanisms. Similarly, Bakker (2007) analyzes the politics of re-municipalization in water and energy sectors, showing how communities have reclaimed collective control over essential services following periods of neoliberal privatization, thereby creating spaces for experimentation with democratic economic governance.

Closely related to this perspective, recent work on economic democracy has expanded the analytical scope of democratic ownership beyond the level of the individual firm. Scholars such as Cumbers, alongside contributions from critical economic geography, have examined how collective ownership structures can be embedded within broader regional development strategies, reshaping spatial inequalities and reconfiguring relations between capital, labor, and the state (Cumbers, 2018; Gibson-Graham, 2006b). This literature highlights the territorial and political dimensions of ownership, emphasizing that democratization of the economy is not merely a question of internal firm governance but also of scale, coordination, and public purpose. Atzeni and Ghigliani (2012) extends this analysis by examining recuperated enterprises in Latin America, demonstrating how worker takeovers of bankrupt firms generate new forms of territorial solidarity and challenge conventional boundaries between economic and political struggle.

The spatial dimension of economic alternatives has received particular attention from scholars working at the intersection of geography and political economy. Fuller et al. (2010) explores the diverse economies approach, which seeks to make visible and strengthen non-capitalist economic practices already embedded within capitalist spaces—from informal economies to gift relations and commons-based production. This analytical perspective challenges the totalizing rhetoric that presents capitalism as an all-encompassing system, instead revealing the heterogeneity and incompleteness of actually existing economic arrangements. North (2007) complements this work by examining how alternative economic spaces—such as social enterprises, community currencies, and local exchange trading systems—can function as sites of prefigurative politics, embodying post-capitalist values even while remaining constrained by capitalist market imperatives.

Debates on market socialism have likewise been revitalized, challenging the widespread assumption that market-based coordination necessarily reproduces capitalist social relations. Authors such as Burczak and Ellerman, drawing in different ways on post-Hayekian insights, argue that systems combining social or worker ownership with markets may constitute a genuine systemic alternative rather than a merely reformist accommodation (Burczak, 2006; Ellerman, 1990). Schweickart (2011b) develops a comprehensive model of "economic democracy" that combines worker self-management, socialized investment, and market allocation of goods and services, arguing that such a system can overcome both the inefficiencies of central planning and the inequities of capitalism. At the same time, critics have noted that market socialist arrangements may struggle to escape competitive imperatives and the commodification of social life (Wright, 2010b). McNally (1993) argues that market coordination tends to reproduce alienation and exploitation even under conditions of collective ownership, as competitive pressures compel worker-owned firms to behave in ways analogous to capitalist enterprises. Reflecting this tension, this book does not treat market socialism as a unified or internally coherent model. Instead, it approaches market socialist experiments as empirical and theoretical sites through which to examine the frictions between institutional transformation and the persistence of commodified everyday social relations.

The relationship between markets and democracy in post-capitalist alternatives has also been examined through the lens of institutional pluralism. Polanyi (2001b) reminds us that markets are always embedded within broader social and political institutions, suggesting that the question is not whether to use markets but how they are regulated, for whose benefit, and according to what logics of justification. Bowles and Gintis (2012) develops this insight further by analyzing how economic systems combining cooperative ownership, participatory planning, and regulated markets might generate substantively different outcomes than both capitalism and command economies, particularly regarding the distribution of power and the quality of democratic participation.

These contemporary debates also echo earlier theoretical discussions concerning reform, revolution, and the role of the state in processes of social transformation. In particular, Poulantzas's analysis of the capitalist state and his critique of both reformist gradualism and insurrectionary rupture remain influential reference points for understanding the strategic dilemmas faced by transformative projects operating within existing institutional frameworks (Poulantzas, 1978). More recent statetheoretical work has further emphasized the contradictory and relational nature of state power, highlighting both the constraints and openings that confront projects of radical institutional change (Jessop, 2002). Panitch and Gindin (2013) extends this analysis by examining how left governments attempting radical transformation within democratic frameworks face structural pressures from capital mobility, financial markets, and international institutions, necessitating strategic thinking about how to build counter-hegemonic power while managing these constraints.

The question of transition strategies has generated particularly productive debates. Wright (2010b) proposes a tripartite framework distinguishing between ruptural, interstitial, and symbiotic transformation strategies, each operating according to different logics and timeframes. Interstitial strategies build alternative institutions within capitalism's interstices, symbiotic strategies use state power to reshape capitalist institutions in democracy-enhancing directions, while ruptural strategies seek sharp breaks with existing structures. Wainwright (2018) critiques this typology as insufficiently attentive to the dynamics of political contestation, arguing that transformative politics requires sustained attention to movement building, ideological struggle, and the cultivation of democratic capacities that cannot be reduced to institutional design alone.

Finally, a range of adjacent traditions have expanded the landscape of postcapitalist thought by shifting attention toward social reproduction, everyday life, and non-capitalist value systems. Work on the foundational economy has emphasized the centrality of mundane infrastructures and collective provisioning systems—such as housing, utilities, care, and transport—in sustaining social life and economic resilience (Foundational Economy Collective, 2019). Bayliss et al. (2020) develops this approach by demonstrating how universal basic services could provide a foundation for post-capitalist transformation, decommodifying essential dimensions of social reproduction while building solidaristic political constituencies. The centrality of care work and social reproduction to any viable post-capitalist alternative has been forcefully articulated by feminist political economists (Fraser & Jaeggi, 2018), who argue that capitalist crisis is fundamentally rooted in contradictions between accumulation and social reproduction, suggesting that alternatives must be organized around principles of care, interdependence, and ecological sustainability rather than competitive individualism.

Post-colonial and decolonial perspectives, including Buen Vivir and related Indigenous cosmologies, have further challenged Eurocentric assumptions about development, growth, and human flourishing, foregrounding relational notions of wellbeing and ecological embeddedness (Gudynas, 2011; Escobar, 2018). Acosta (2013) elaborates how Buen Vivir represents not merely an alternative development model but an alternative to development itself, prioritizing harmony with nature, community solidarity, and cultural diversity over extractivism and endless accumulation. Coulthard (2014) extends this critique through an analysis of Indigenous resurgence movements, demonstrating how struggles for land, self-determination, and cultural survival challenge the colonial foundations of capitalist modernity. These perspectives intersect productively with degrowth scholarship (D'Alisa et al., 2014; Hickel, 2020), which questions the compatibility of infinite economic expansion with ecological limits and social well-being, proposing instead economies oriented toward sufficiency, conviviality, and democratic deliberation about collective needs.

While these approaches are not the primary focus of this book, they underscore the breadth of contemporary efforts to imagine economic systems oriented toward social reproduction, autonomy, and collective well-being rather than accumulation alone. They also highlight the necessity of situating debates about economic alternatives within broader questions of ecological sustainability, social justice, and the decolonization of political imagination. Any adequate theorization of post-capitalist futures must grapple with the entanglement of economic structures with systems of racialized exploitation, gendered oppression, and ecological devastation—recognizing that transformation requires not merely institutional redesign but fundamental reorientations in how human communities understand their relationships to each other and to the more-than-human world.

Rather than offering a competing institutional blueprint, this book contributes to these debates by foregrounding a Situationist concern with everyday life, lived autonomy, and the experiential dimensions of social transformation. By evaluating contemporary reforms and alternative models through this lens, it complements existing political economy approaches while extending the analysis to questions of time, activity, and subjectivity that are often left implicit in institutional and policycentered accounts of post-capitalist futures.

The case of Iceland is a paradigmatic example of the strategic use of institutional frameworks for emancipatory ends. The working time reduction was presented not as an instrument for productivity or business efficiency, but as a profound re-evaluation of the role of work in human life, connecting temporal liberation with broader goals of gender equality, environmental sustainability, and democratic participation. This approach demonstrates that institutional reforms can generate transformative effects if they are strategically articulated with social demands and broader movements, functioning as catalysts for critical reflection and collective action.

Mondragón, for its part, provides evidence that reforms should not be limited to improving immediate conditions but must build collective capabilities and organizational skills that enable sustained democratic participation and economic cooperation. The cooperative network has shown how technical and civic education, combined with democratic governance practices, can become a laboratory for social transformation, even within capitalist structures and in the face of competitive pressures.

Among the key strategies to enhance the transformative capacity of reforms and prevent their cooptation are:

Integrating reforms within broader social movements that maintain political pressure and constant mobilization, preventing isolated gains from being neutralized or institutionalized in ways that reinforce the dominant logic.

Designing reforms to increase the organizational and action capacity of grassroots movements, strengthening the autonomy of the actors involved and the resilience of social mobilization.

Leveraging educational and training institutions to develop technical skills, critical consciousness, and democratic practices, ensuring the long-term sustainability and continuity of changes.

Building international solidarity networks that can resist the pressure of capital and global market dynamics, facilitating the adaptation and scaling of local innovations to different contexts.

The study recognizes the limitations of generalizing the analyzed cases due to the contextual specificity of Iceland and Mondragón, including cultural, institutional, economic, and political factors that may not be easily replicable in other countries or regions. However, it proposes that transformative reforms must be built on existing cultural and institutional resources, adapting successful practices to local contexts rather than literally transplanting foreign models. This approach emphasizes the need for a situated approach that respects local conditions and leverages cultural and institutional strengths to maximize transformative potential.

The developed analytical framework, based on Situationist concepts such as spectacle, alienation, institutional *détournement*, and spatial reappropriation, allows for an evaluation of whether reforms tend to reinforce or subvert the logic of the spectacle. This perspective avoids binary classifications of success/failure and provides tools to measure degrees of transformation, considering material, symbolic, and cultural effects. By focusing on the interaction between institutional action and social consciousness, this framework facilitates a more nuanced understanding of how reforms can contribute to significant social changes.

The adoption of a dialectical and multi-methodological approach is a central element of the research, combining quantitative analysis of outcomes with a qualitative evaluation of lived experiences, cultural practices, and political consciousness. This methodological combination allows for an understanding of how reforms can simultaneously reproduce and challenge existing social relations, revealing tensions and contradictions that are essential for planning transformative interventions.

In terms of political and social implications, the study suggests that institutional reforms can serve as platforms to strengthen worker autonomy, democratize decisionmaking spaces, and foster social solidarity and environmental sustainability. The key is to structure these interventions in a way that expands collective capacities and promotes authentic experiences of participation, preventing cooptation from reducing reforms to mere functional improvements within the dominant system.

Finally, the study's conclusions point toward future lines of research: a comparative evaluation of how different institutional reforms can generate transformative effects in diverse cultural, economic, and political contexts; an analysis of specific cooptation mechanisms and resistance strategies; and a study of the interaction between local reforms and transnational solidarity networks as key factors for the sustainability of changes. It is also recommended to explore how Situationist approaches can continue to inform the planning of innovative reforms, ensuring they contribute to social emancipation, equity, and environmental justice in the long term.

In summary, although institutional reforms alone do not constitute revolutionary praxis, they can create conditions of possibility for profound social transformations if they are strategically integrated with social movements, education, international solidarity, and cooptation resistance strategies. The challenge lies in maintaining a dialectical, multi-methodological, and contextualized approach that allows for maximizing transformative impacts while recognizing and managing inherent structural and temporal limitations.

Bibliography

Acosta, A. (2013). *El Buen Vivir: Sumak Kawsay, una oportunidad para imaginar otros mundos.* Icaria.

Adorno, T. W., & Horkheimer, M. (2002). *Dialectic of enlightenment.* Stanford University Press.

Aglietta, M. (1979). *A theory of capitalist regulation.* New Left Books.

Akerlof, G. A. (1986). Labor contracts as partial gift exchange. *The Quarterly Journal of Economics.*

Akuno, K., & Nangwaya, A. (Eds.). (2017). *Jackson rising: The struggle for economic democracy and black self-determination in Jackson, Mississippi.* Daraja Press.

Albert, M. (2003). *Parecon: Life after capitalism.* Verso.

Alperovitz, G. (2016). *What then must we do? Straight talk about the next American Revolution.* Chelsea Green.

Antal, M., Plank, B., Mokter, M., & Fuchs, D. (2020). Time for degrowth? Exploring the temporal dimension in degrowth discourse. *Journal of Cleaner Production.*

Arando, S., Freundlich, F., Gago, M., Jones, D. C., & Kato, T. (2015). Happiness at work in worker cooperatives. *Labour Economics.*

Arrieta, K. I., Santos, G. M., & Alzola, M. A. (2018). Worker commitment in mondragon worker cooperatives. *Economic and Industrial Democracy.*

Atkinson, A. B. (2015). *Inequality: What can be done?* Harvard University Press.

Atzeni, M., & Ghigliani, P. (2012). *Labour process and decision-making in factories under workers' self-management: Empirical evidence from Argentina.* Brill.

M. Brum, *Democratic Alternatives*,
https://doi.org/10.1007/978-3-032-23153-6

Ayadi, R., Llewellyn, D. T., Schmidt, R. H., Arbak, E., & De Groen, W. P. (2010). *Investigating diversity in the banking sector in Europe: The performance and role of savings banks*. CEPS.

Azkarraga, J., Cheney, G., & Udaondo, A. (2012). Mondragón's educational innovation: Cooperative learning and knowledge management. *Cooperative Education*.

Baiocchi, G. (2005). *Militants and citizens: The politics of participatory democracy in Porto Alegre*. Stanford University Press.

Bakaikoa, B., Errasti, A., & Begiristain, A. (2017). Financial crisis and solidarity within Mondragón cooperative group. *Business History*.

Baker, C. (2018). *The cooperative movement: A global view*. Routledge.

Bakker, A. B., & Demerouti, E. (2014). Job demands–resources theory: Taking stock and looking forward. *Journal of Occupational Health Psychology*.

Bakker, K. (2007). The "commons" versus the "commodity": Alter-globalization, anti-privatization and the human right to water in the global south. *Antipode, 39*(3), 430–455.

Bambra, C. (2021). *The second wave: How the pandemic revealed the crisis of our health system*. Policy Press.

Bardhan, P. K., & Roemer, J. E. (Eds.). (1993). *Market socialism: The current debate*. Oxford University Press.

Basterretxea, I., & Albizu, E. (2019). Cooperative identity and human resource management: The Mondragón case. *Human Resource Management Journal*.

Bauwens, M. (2005). The political economy of peer production. *Post-Autistic Economics Review*.

Bauwens, M., Kostakis, V., & Pazaitis, A. (2019). *Peer to peer: The commons manifesto*. University of Westminster Press.

Bayliss, K., & Van Waeyenberge, E. (2020). *The political economy of development: The world bank, neoliberalism and development research*. Pluto Press.

Bell, D. (1973). *The coming of post-industrial society*. Basic Books.

Benjamin, W. (1968a). *The author as producer*. New Left Review.

Benjamin, W. (1968b). *Theses on the philosophy of history*. Schocken Books.

Benkler, Y. (2006). *The wealth of networks: How social production transforms markets and freedom*. Yale University Press.

Berardi, F. (2009). *The soul at work: From alienation to autonomy*. Semiotext(e).

Berg, J., Furrer, M., Harmon, E., Rani, U., & Silberman, M. S. (2021). *Reducing working hours as a climate policy: An analysis of barriers and opportunities*. International Labour Organization.

Bernstein, E. (1899). *Evolutionary socialism*. Independent Labour Party.

Best, S., & Kellner, D. (1997). *The postmodern turn*. Guilford Press.

Birchall, J., & Hammond Ketilson, L. (2013). *The resilience of the cooperative business model in times of crisis*. ILO.

Boltanski, L., & Chiapello, E. (2005). *The new spirit of capitalism*. Verso.
Bourguignon, F., Ferreira, F. H., & Lustig, N. (Eds.). (2015). *The handbook of income distribution*. Elsevier.
Bowles, S., & Gintis, H. (2011). *A cooperative species: Human reciprocity and its evolution*. Princeton University Press.
Bowles, S., & Gintis, H. (2012). *A cooperative species: Human reciprocity and its evolution*. Princeton University Press.
Brandt, T., & Schulten, T. (2019). *The Nordic labour relations model at a crossroads*. ETUI.
Brandt, T., Schulten, T., & Müller, T. (2021). *Working time policy between flexibility and worker protection*. ETUI.
Brandth, B., & Kvande, E. (2012). Masculinities and the gender revolution: The transformation of modern. Societies. *Sociology Compass*.
Brecht, B. (1964). *Brecht on theatre: The development of an aesthetic*. Hill and Wang.
Breines, W. (1982). *Community and organization in the New Left, 1962–1968: The great refusal*. Praeger.
Brenner, N. (2009). What is critical urban theory? *City*.
Bretos, I., Errasti, A., & Marcuello, C. (2018). Challenges and opportunities for the regeneration of multinational worker cooperatives: Lessons from the Fagor. Experience. *Organization*.
Bretos, I., Errasti, A., & Marcuello, C. (2019). Cooperative networks and social innovation: How Mondragón pioneers collaborative advantage. *Innovation: Management, Policy & Practice*.
Brown, E. H. (2013). *The public bank solution: From austerity to prosperity*. Third Millennium Press, Baton Rouge.
Brown, P. (2019). *The refusal of work: The theory and practice of resistance to work*. Zed Books.
Buchanan, J. M., & Tullock, G. (1962). *The Calculus of Consent: Logical Foundations of Constitutional Democracy*. University of Michigan Press.
Buch-Hansen, H. (2021). *Public wealth: How we can save our common resources*. Edward Elgar.
Buch-Hansen, H., & Koch, M. (2018). *Universal Basic Income: A Progressive Policy for the Twenty-First Century?* Edward Elgar.
Buck-Morss, S. (1992). *The dialectics of seeing: Walter Benjamin and the Arcades Project*. MIT Press.
Burczak, T. (2006). *Socialism after Hayek*. University of Michigan Press.
Burkett, P. (1999). *Marx and nature: A red and green perspective. St.* Martin's Press.
Calleja-López, A., Monterde, A., & Barandiaran, X. (2017). Participatory democracy enhanced: The case of decidim platform. *Social Internet of Things*.

Castles, F. G. (1978). *The social democratic image of society.* Routledge & Kegan Paul.

Cette, G., Chouard, V., & Verdugo, G. (2013a). Reducing the length of the working week: What have we learned? *World Economics.*

Cette, G., Chouard, V., & Verdugo, G. (2013b). *Working time reductions: French lessons for Korea.* Korea Development Institute.

Cheney, G. (1999). *Values at work: Employee participation meets market pressure at Mondragon.* ILR Press.

Chiapello, E. (2007). The new spirit of capitalism. *International Journal of Politics, Culture, and Society.*

Clark, G. L., & Monk, A. H. (2008). *The world's biggest investors: A trillion dollar question.* Watson Wyatt Worldwide.

Clark, P., & Mikami, Y. (2019). *Rethinking institutional banking: A blueprint for financial cooperatives.* Edward Elgar.

Cleaver, H. (1979). *Reading capital politically.* University of Texas Press.

Coote, A., Harper, A., & Stirling, A. (2021). *The case for a four day week.* Polity Press.

Cornforth, C., Thomas, A., Lewis, J., & Spear, R. (1995). *Patterns of cooperative management.* Paul Chapman.

Coulthard, G. S. (2014). *Red skin, white masks: Rejecting the colonial politics of recognition.* University of Minnesota Press.

Craig, J. (1993). *The heart of the matter: Worker cooperatives and labor solidarity in the new world order.* Black Rose Books.

Creswell, J. W., & Creswell, J. D. (2017). *Research design: Qualitative, quantitative, and mixed methods approaches.* Sage Publications.

Cross, G. (1988). *God's day: A history of leisure and work in industrial America.* Temple University Press.

Cumbers, A. (2018). *Reclaiming public ownership: Making space for economic democracy.* Zed Books.

D'Alisa, G., Demaria, F., & Kallis, G. (Eds.). (2014). *Degrowth: A vocabulary for a new era.* Routledge.

Davis, A. Y. (1981). *Women, race, and class.* Random House.

Davis, J. E. (Ed.). (2010). *The community land trust reader.* Lincoln Institute of Land Policy.

Day, R. J. F. (2005). *Gramsci is dead: Anarchist currents in the newest social movements.* Pluto Press.

De Beistegui, M., & Ross, A. (Eds.). (2018). *The situationist international: A critical handbook.* Pluto Press.

Debord, G. (1955). Introduction to a critique of urban geography. *Les Lèvres Nues*, 6.

Debord, G. (1956). Theory of the dérive. *Internationale Situationniste, 2*, 50–54.

Debord, G. (1967). *The society of the spectacle.* Buchet-Chastel.
Debord, G. (1970). *The society of the spectacle* (Rev. ed.). Black & Red.
Debord, G. (1994). *The society of the spectacle.* Zone Books. Reprint of the 1967 edition.
Debord, G. (1995). *The society of the spectacle* (Rev. ed.). Zone Books.
Debord, G., & Wolman, G. J. (1956). A user's guide to détournement. *Les Lèvres Nues*, 8.
Deleuze, G., & Guattari, F. (1977). *Anti-Oedipus: Capitalism and Schizophrenia.* University of Minnesota Press.
DiMaggio, P. J., & Powell, W. W. (1983). The iron cage revisited: Institutional isomorphism and collective rationality in organizational fields. *American Sociological Review.*
Ellerman, D. (1990). *The democratic worker-owned firm.* Unwin Hyman.
Errasti, A., Heras, I., Bakaikoa, B., & Elgoibar, P. (2013). Mondragón's Chinese subsidiaries: Cooperatives promoting economic and social development. *World Development.*
Escobar, A. (2018). *Designs for the pluriverse: Radical interdependence, autonomy, and the making of worlds.* Duke University Press.
Esping-Andersen, G. (1990). *The three worlds of welfare capitalism.* Princeton University Press.
Federici, S. (2012). *Revolution at point zero: Housework, reproduction, and feminist struggle.* PM Press.
Ferri, G., Kalmi, P., & Kerola, E. (2014). *The role of cooperative banks in the financial crisis.* Edward Elgar.
Fioramonti, L. (2017). *Wellbeing economics: A new economics for the 21st century.* Palgrave Macmillan.
Fitzgerald, J., & Wray, L. R. (2019). *Greening the economy through shorter working hours.* Political Economy Research Institute.
Flyvbjerg, B. (2006). Five misunderstandings about case-study research. *Qualitative Inquiry.*
Folbre, N. (2001). *The invisible heart: Economics and family values.* The New Press.
Foster, J. B. (2009). *The ecological revolution: Making peace with the planet.* Monthly Review Press.
Foundational Economy Collective. (2019). *Foundational economy: The infrastructure of everyday life.* Manchester University Press.
Fourier, C. (1996). *The theory of the four movements.* Cambridge University Press.
Fraser, N. (1994). After the family wage: Gender equity and the welfare state. *Political Theory.*
Fraser, N. (2013). *Fortunes of feminism: From state-managed capitalism to neoliberal crisis.* Verso.

Fraser, N. (2022). *Cannibal capitalism: How our system is devouring democracy, care, and the planet—and what we can do about it.* Verso.
Fraser, N., & Jaeggi, R. (2018). *Capitalism: A conversation in critical theory.* Polity Press.
Frayne, D. (2019). *The refusal of work: The theory and practice of resistance to work.* Zed Books.
Freire, P. (2000). *Pedagogy of the oppressed.* Continuum.
Friedman, M. (1962). *Capitalism and freedom.* University of Chicago Press.
Fuchs, C. (2014). *Digital labour and Karl Marx.* Routledge.
Fuller, D., Jonas, A. E. G., & Lee, R. (2010). Interrogating alterity: Alternative economic and political spaces. *Geoforum, 41*(6), 311–315.
Gibson-Graham, J. K. (2006a). *A postcapitalist politics.* University of Minnesota Press.
Gibson-Graham, J. K. (2006b). *A postcapitalist politics.* University of Minnesota Press.
Gibson-Graham, J. K., Cameron, J., & Healy, S. (2013). *Take back the economy: An ethical guide for transforming our communities.* University of Minnesota Press.
Giddens, A. (1998). *The third way: The renewal of social democracy.* Polity Press.
Gilmore, R. W. (2007). *Golden gulag: Prisons, surplus, crisis, and opposition in globalizing California.* University of California Press.
Gitlin, T. (2012). *Occupy nation: The roots, the spirit, and the promise of occupy wall street.* itBooks.
Golden, L. (2012a). The economics of working time: An introduction and survey. *Journal of Economic Surveys.*
Golden, L. (Ed.). (2012b). *Working time: International trends, theory and policy perspectives.* Routledge.
Goldsmith, S. (2010). *Alaska's Dividend: A model for the world.* Basic Income Earth Network.
González, S., & Marcuello, C. (2020). The limits of cooperative development: Market constraints and organizational tensions. *Economic and Industrial Democracy.*
Gornick, J. C., & Meyers, M. K. (2003). *Families that work: Policies for reconciling parenthood and employment.* Russell Sage Foundation.
Gorz, A. (1967). *Strategy for labor: A radical proposal.* Beacon Press.
Gorz, A. (1968). *Strategy for labor: A radical proposal.* Beacon Press.
Gorz, A. (1989). *Critique of economic reason.* Verso.
Gorz, A. (1999). *Reclaiming work: Beyond the wage-based society.* Polity Press.
Graeber, D. (2009). *Direct action: An ethnography.* AK Press.
Gramsci, A. (1971). *Selections from the prison notebooks.* International Publishers.

Greenwood, D., & González Santos, J. L. (2019). The spatial dimensions of Mondragón: Cooperative networks and regional development. *Regional Studies.*

Gudynas, E. (2011). Buen vivir: Today's tomorrow. *Development, 54*(4), 441–447.

Guinan, J., & O'Neill, M. (2019). *The case for community wealth building.* Polity Press.

Habermas, J. (1987). *The theory of communicative action, volume 2: Lifeworld and System: A critique of functionalist reason.* Beacon Press.

Hahnel, R. (2005). *Economic justice and democracy: From competition to cooperation.* Routledge.

Hall, P. A., & Soskice, D. (Eds.). (2001). *Varieties of capitalism: The institutional foundations of comparative advantage.* Oxford University Press.

Hanisch, C. (1970). The personal is political. *Notes from the Second. Year: Women's Liberation*, 76–78.

Hanna, T. M. (2018). *Our common wealth: The return of public ownership in the United States.* Manchester University Press.

Hansmann, H. (1996). *The ownership of enterprise.* Harvard University Press.

Haraldsson, G. D., & Kellam, J. (2021). *Going public: Iceland's journey to a shorter working week* (Technical Report). Autonomy and Association for Sustainable Democracy in Iceland.

Hardt, M., & Negri, A. (2000). *Empire.* Harvard University Press.

Harvey, D. (1989). *The condition of postmodernity.* Blackwell.

Harvey, D. (2000). *Spaces of hope.* University of California Press.

Harvey, D. (2005). *A brief history of neoliberalism.* Oxford University Press.

Harvey, D. (2008). *The right to the city.* New Left Review.

Harvey, D. (2012). *Rebel cities: From the right to the city to the urban revolution.* Verso.

Haushofer, J., & Shapiro, J. (2016). The short-term impact of unconditional cash transfers to the poor: Experimental evidence from kenya (Technical Report). *The Quarterly Journal of Economics.*

Hayden, A. (2006). Shorter work time as a path to full employment. *Progressive Planning.*

Hayek, F. A. (1944). *The road to Serfdom.* University of Chicago Press.

Hayek, F. A. (1945). The use of knowledge in society. *American Economic Review.*

Hayes, M. T. (2022). *Beyond the welfare state: The new political economy of welfare.* Palgrave Macmillan.

Heath, J., & Potter, A. (2004). *Nation of rebels: Why counterculture became consumer culture.* HarperBusiness.

Held, D. (2004). *Global covenant: The social democratic alternative to the Washington consensus.* Polity Press.

Hempel, L. M. (2022). *Time, gender and the division of labour: The significance of caring*. Edward Elgar.

Heras-Saizarbitoria, I. (2016). Organizational innovation in worker cooperatives: The Mondragón case. *International Review of Sociology*.

Hickel, J. (2020). *Less is more: How degrowth will save the world*. Penguin Random House.

Hinrichs, K., Roche, W. K., & Sirianni, C. (1991). *Working time in transition: The political economy of working hours in industrial nations*. Temple University Press.

Hochschild, A. R. (2012). *The outsourced self: Intimate life in market times*. Metropolitan Books.

Holloway, J. (2002). *Change the world without taking power: The meaning of revolution today*. Pluto Press.

Hooks, B. (1994). *Outlaw culture: Resisting representations*. Routledge.

Huizinga, J. (1955). *Homo Ludens: A study of the play-element in culture*. Beacon Press.

Hussey, A. (2001). *The game of war: The life and death of guy debord*. Jonathan Cape.

Inglehart, R. (1997). *Modernization and postmodernization: Cultural, economic, and political change in 43 societies*. Princeton University Press.

International Co-operative Alliance. (2018). *Blueprint for a Co-operative Decade*. ICA.

Isaac, T. T., & Franke, R. W. (2005). *Planning for empowerment: The political economy of participatory budgeting in Kerala, India*. Left Word.

Jackson, B. (2007). *Social democracy in global context: The origins and development during the golden age*. Oxford University Press.

Jackson, T. (2017). *Prosperity without growth: Foundations for the economy of tomorrow*. Routledge.

Jappe, A. (1999). *Guy debord*. University of California Press.

Jessop, B. (2002). *The future of the capitalist state*. Polity Press.

Judt, T. (2005). *Postwar: A history of Europe since 1945*. Penguin Press.

Kallis, G. (2018). *Degrowth*. Columbia University Press.

Kangas, O., Jauhiainen, S., Simanainen, M., & Ylikännö, M. (2019). The basic income experiment 2017–2018 in finland: Preliminary results (Technical Report). Ministry of Social Affairs and Health.

Kasmir, S. (1996). *The myth of Mondragón: Cooperatives, politics, and working-class life in a Basque town*. SUNY Press.

Katzenstein, P. J. (1985). *Small states in world markets: Industrial policy in Europe*. Cornell University Press.

Kellner, D. (2003). *Media spectacle*. Routledge.

Keynes, J. M. (1930). *Economic possibilities for our grandchildren*. Macmillan.

Keynes, J. M. (1936). *The general theory of employment, interest and money.* Macmillan.

Kitschelt, H. (1994). *The transformation of European social democracy.* Cambridge University Press.

Klein, N. (2014). *This changes everything: Capitalism Vs. The Climate.* Simon & Schuster.

Knabb, K. (2006). *Situationist international anthology.* Bureau of Public Secrets.

Knight, P. T. (2012). Working with the grain? the cooperative principles as a source of social capital. *Journal of Co-operative Organization and. Management, 2*(2), 126–133.

Kornai, J. (1992). *The socialist system: The political economy of communism.* Princeton University Press.

Korpi, W. (1983). *The democratic class struggle.* Routledge & Kegan Paul.

Korpi, W. (2002). The great trough in unemployment: A long-term view of unemployment, inflation strikes, and the profit/wage ratio. *Politics & Society.*

Koslowski, A., Blum, S., Dobrotic, I., Kaufman, G., & Moss, P. (2022). *Working time in European welfare states.* Policy Press.

Kotanyi, A., & Vaneigem, R. (1961). Elementary program of the bureau of unitary urbanism. *Internationale Situationniste*, 6.

Kovel, J. (2007). *The enemy of nature: The end of capitalism or the end of the world?* Zed Books.

Krugman, P. (2009). *The return of depression economics and the crisis of 2008.* W. W. Norton.

Laing, R. (1967). *The politics of experience.* Pantheon Books.

Lange, O., & Taylor, F. M. (1938). *On the economic theory of socialism.* University of Minnesota Press.

Lareau, A. (2011). *Unequal childhoods: Class, race, and family life.* University of California Press.

Lavoie, D. (1985). *Rivalry and central planning: The socialist calculation debate reconsidered.* Cambridge University Press.

Lazzarato, M. (1996). *Immaterial labor.* Red Notes.

Lebowitz, M. A. (2012). *The contradictions of "Real Socialism": The conductor and the conducted.* Monthly Review Press.

Lefebvre, H. (1968). *Le Droit À la Ville.* Anthropos.

Lefebvre, H. (1991a). *Critique of everyday life.* Verso.

Lefebvre, H. (1991b). *The production of space.* Blackwell.

Lefebvre, H. (1996). *Writings on cities.* Blackwell.

Lehndorff, S. (2014). *Divisive integration: The triumph of failed ideas in Europe-revisited.* ETUI.

Lewis, J. (1992). Gender and the development of welfare regimes. *Journal of European Social Policy.*

Lipietz, A. (1987). *Mirages and miracles: The crisis of global fordism*. Verso.

Löwy, M. (2018). *Ecosocialism: A radical alternative to capitalist catastrophe*. Haymarket Books.

Lukács, G. (1971). *History and class consciousness*. MIT Press.

Macpherson, C. B. (1977). *The life and times of liberal democracy*. Oxford University Press.

Mahoney, J., & Goertz, G. (2012). *A tale of two cultures: Qualitative and quantitative research in the social sciences*. Princeton University Press.

Maier, C. S. (1987). *In search of stability: Explorations in historical political economy*. Cambridge University Press.

Marcus, G. (1989). *Lipstick traces: A secret history of the twentieth century*. Harvard University Press.

Marcuse, H. (1955). *Eros and civilization: A philosophical inquiry into freud*. Beacon Press.

Marcuse, H. (1969). *One-dimensional man: Studies in the ideology of advanced industrial society*. Beacon Press.

Marshall, T. (1950). *Citizenship and social class*. Cambridge University Press.

Marx, K. (1976). *Capital: A critique of political economy (Vol 1)*. Penguin.

Mason, P. (2012). *Why it's kicking off everywhere: The new global revolutions*. Verso.

Mazzucato, M. (2020). *The value of everything: Making and taking in the global economy*. PublicAffairs.

Mazzucato, M. (2021). *Mission economy: A moonshot guide to changing capitalism*. Harper Business.

McAdam, D. (1999). *Political process and the development of black insurgency, 1930–1970*. University of Chicago Press.

McCarthy, O., Briscoe, R., & Ward, M. (2019). *Cooperatives in a global economy: The challenge of competition*. Edward Elgar.

McDowell, L. (2004). *Debord and the situationists*. Reaktion Books.

McNally, D. (1993). *Against the market: Political economy, market socialism and the marxist critique*. Verso.

Meil, P., & Henselek, Y. (2017). *Working time, health and safety: A research synthesis paper*. European Agency for Safety and Health at Work.

Mendonça, M., Lacey, S., & Hvelplund, F. (2009). *Feed-in tariffs: Accelerating the deployment of renewable energy*. Earthscan.

Merchant, C. (1980). *The death of nature: Women, ecology, and the scientific revolution*. Harper & Row.

Merrifield, A. (2005). *Guy debord*. Reaktion Books.

Michels, R. (1915). *Political parties: A sociological study of the oligarchical tendencies of modern democracy*. The Free Press.

Mies, M., & Bennholdt-Thomsen, V. (1997). *The subsistence perspective: Beyond the globalised economy*. Zed Books.

Miller, D. (1989). *Market, state, and community: Theoretical foundations of market socialism*. Clarendon Press.

Mitchell, C. (2016). *Community broadband networks*. Institute for Local Self-Reliance.

Molina, F., & MacLeod, G. (2020). *Origins and evolution of the Mondragón experiment*. Palgrave Macmillan.

Moore, S. A., & Wilson, J. (2018). Tactical urbanism: Short-term action for long-term change. *Journal of Planning Education and Research*.

Morgan, K. (2004). Collective learning and knowledge development in the evolution of regional high technology complexes. *Regional Studies*.

New Economics Foundation. (2021). *Time for change: Flexible working and wellbeing* (Technical Report). New Economics Foundation.

North, P. (2007). Money and liberation: The micropolitics of alternative currency movements. *Cultural Studies, 21*(4–5), 632–649.

Notes from Nowhere. (2002). *One no, many yeses: A journey to the heart of the global resistance movement*. Verso.

Nove, A. (1983). *The economics of feasible socialism*. George Allen & Unwin.

O'Connor, J. (1973). *The fiscal crisis of the state*. St Martin's Press.

Offe, C. (1984). *Contradictions of the welfare state*. MIT Press.

Ostrom, E. (1990). *Governing the commons: The evolution of institutions for collective action*. Cambridge University Press.

Panitch, L., & Gindin, S. (2013). *The making of global capitalism: The political Economy of American Empire*. Verso.

Pannekoek, A. (1948). *Workers' councils*. AK Press.

Pateman, C. (1970). *Participation and democratic theory*. Cambridge University Press.

Pateman, C. (1988). *The sexual contract*. Polity Press.

Pateman, C. (2012). Participatory democracy revisited. *Perspectives on Politics*.

Pencavel, J. (2015). The productivity of working hours. *The Economic Journal*.

Pencavel, J., Pistaferri, L., & Schivardi, F. (2012). *Worker participation: Lessons from the worker co-ops of the Pacific Northwest*. Russell Sage Foundation.

Pettifor, A. (2019). *The case for the green new deal*. Verso.

Piketty, T. (2014). *Capital in the twenty-first century*. Harvard University Press.

Pine, B. J., & Gilmore, J. H. (1999). *The experience economy*. Harvard Business School Press.

Piven, F. F. (2006). *Challenging authority: How ordinary people change America*. Rowman & Littlefield.

Piven, F. F., & Cloward, R. A. (2009). *Poor people's movements: Why they succeed, how they fail*. Vintage Books.

Plant, S. (1992). *The most radical gesture: The situationist international in a postmodern age*. Routledge.

Polanyi, K. (2001a). *The great transformation: The political and economic origins of our time*. Beacon Press.

Polanyi, K. (2001b). *The great transformation: The political and economic origins of our time* (2nd ed.). Beacon Press. (Original work published 1944).

Pontusson, J. (2011). Once and future social democracy. *Annual Review of Political Science*.

Poulantzas, N. (1978). *State, power, socialism*. Verso.

Przeworski, A. (1985). *Capitalism and social democracy*. Cambridge University Press.

Pullinger, M. (2014). *Working time reduction policy in a sustainable economy: Criteria and options for its design*. Ecological Economics.

Putnam, R. D. (2000). *Bowling alone: The collapse and revival of American Community*. Simon & Schuster.

Putnam, R. D. (2007). *Bowling alone: The collapse and revival of American Community*. Simon & Schuster.

Ragin, C. C. (2000). *Fuzzy-set social science*. University of Chicago Press.

Reason, P., & Bradbury, H. (Eds.). (2008). *The SAGE handbook of action research: Participative inquiry and practice*. SAGE Publications.

Restakis, J. (2010). *Humanizing the economy: Co-operatives in the age of capital*. New Society Publishers.

Robinson, C. J. (2000). *Black Marxism: The making of the black radical tradition*. University of North Carolina Press.

Rodriguez, M., & Chen, L. (2021). Working time and the future of work. *International Labour Review*.

Roediger, D. R., & Foner, P. S. (1986). *The eight-hour day movement*. University of Illinois Press.

Roemer, J. E. (1994a). *Egalitarian perspectives: Essays in philosophical economics*. Cambridge University Press.

Roemer, J. E. (1994b). *A future for socialism*. Harvard University Press.

Roemer, J. E. (1996). *Equal shares: Making market socialism work*. Verso.

Rosa, H. (2019). *Resonance: A sociology of our relationship to the world*. Polity Press.

Ross, K. (2002). *May'68 and its afterlives*. University of Chicago Press.

Rothschild, J., & Whitt, J. A. (2009). *The cooperative workplace: potentials and dilemmas of organizational democracy and participation*. Cambridge University Press.

Rothschild-Whitt, J. (1979). The collectivist organization: An alternative to rational-bureaucratic models. *American Sociological Review*.

Rothstein, B. (2005). *Social traps and the problem of trust.* Cambridge University Press.

Ruggie, J. G. (1982). International regimes, transactions, and change: Embedded liberalism in the postwar economic order. *International Organization.*

Russell, B. (2019). Participation between democracy and capture: Lessons from the Barcelona En Comú Experience. *European Urban and Regional Studies.*

Russell, J. A. (2012). Participation: The key to cooperative resilience? *Journal of Co-operative Organization and Management, 2*(1), 3–11.

Ryner, J. M. (2002). *Capitalist restructuring, globalisation and the third way: Lessons from the Swedish model.* Routledge.

Sadler, S. (1998). *The situationist city.* MIT Press.

Santos, B. d. S. (Ed.). (2006). *The rise of the global left: The world social forum and beyond.* Zed Books.

Sassoon, D. (1996). *One hundred years of socialism: The West European left in the twentieth century.* New Press.

Scharpf, F. W. (1999). *Governing in Europe: Effective and democratic?* Oxford University Press.

Scholz, T. (2016). *Platform cooperativism: Challenging the corporate sharing economy.* Rosa Luxemburg Stiftung.

Schor, J. B. (1991). *The overworked American: The unexpected decline of leisure.* Basic Books.

Schor, J. B. (2005). Sustainable consumption and worktime reduction. *Journal of Industrial Ecology.*

Schor, J. B. (2010). *Plentitude: The new economics of true wealth.* Penguin Press.

Schweickart, D. (2002). *After capitalism* (1st ed.). Rowman & Littlefield.

Schweickart, D. (2011a). *After capitalism.* Rowman & Littlefield.

Schweickart, D. (2011b). *After capitalism* (2nd ed.). Rowman & Littlefield.

Sen, A. (1999). *Development as freedom.* Knopf.

Siegrist, J., & Li, J. (2017). *Work stress and health in a globalized economy: The model of effort-reward imbalance.* Springer.

Smith, A., Light, A., & Roberts, P. (2020). *Everyday life and the cooperative economy.* Edward Elgar.

Smith, N. (1984). *Uneven development: Nature, capital, and the production of space.* Blackwell.

Southerton, D. (2003). Squeezing time: Allocating practices, coordinating networks and scheduling society. *Time & Society.*

Speth, J. G., & Courrier, P. (Eds.). (2016). *The next system reader: Alternatives to a failed system.* Routledge.

Srnicek, N. (2017). *Platform capitalism.* Polity Press.

Srnicek, N., & Williams, A. (2015). *Inventing the future: Postcapitalism and a world without work.* Verso.

Srnicek, N., & Williams, A. (2017). *Inventing the future: Postcapitalism and a world without work*. Verso.
Standing, G. (2011). *The Precariat: The new dangerous class*. Bloomsbury Academic.
Standing, G. (2017). *Basic income: And how we can make it happen*. Pelican Books.
Stevis, D., & Felli, R. (2018). Just transitions: The politics of green transformation. *Politics & Society*.
Streeck, W. (2014). *Buying time: The delayed crisis of democratic capitalism*. Verso.
Stronge, W. (2019). *Shorter: Work better, live more, save the planet*. Random House Business.
Tarrow, S. (2011). *Power in movement: Social movements and contentious politics*. Cambridge University Press.
Therborn, G. (1995). *European modernity and beyond: The trajectory of European Societies 1945–2000*. Sage.
Thompson, E. (1967). Time, work-discipline, and industrial capitalism. *Past & Present*.
Unger, R. M. (2019). *The knowledge economy*. Verso.
Van Parijs, P., & Vanderborght, Y. (2017). *Basic income: A radical proposal for a free society and a sane economy*. Harvard University Press.
Vaneigem, R. (1967). *The revolution of everyday life*. Left Bank Books.
Vaneigem, R. (1974). *A cavalier history of surrealism*. AK Press.
von Mises, L. (1920). *Economic calculation in the socialist commonwealth*. Auburn University.
Vaneigem, R. (2012). *The revolution of everyday life*. PM Press.
Viénet, R. (1968). *Enragés and situationists in the occupation movement, France, May'68*. Autonomedia.
Wagner, P. (1990). *Social foundations of human experience*. Polity Press.
Wainwright, H. (2018). A new politics from the left. *New Left Review*, *114*, 37–56.
Wampler, B. (2007). *Participatory budgeting in Brazil: Contestation, cooperation, and accountability*. Pennsylvania State University Press.
Weeks, K. (2011). *The problem with work: Feminism, Marxism, antiwork politics, and postwork imaginaries*. Duke University Press.
West, S., Castro Baker, A., Samra, S., & Coltrera, E. (2021). *Preliminary analysis: Seed's first year*. (Technical Report). Center for Guaranteed Income Research.
Whyte, W. F., & Whyte, K. K. (1991). *Making Mondragón: The growth and dynamics of the worker cooperative complex*. ILR Press.
Widerquist, K., & Howard, M. W. (Eds.). (2013). *Alaska's permanent fund dividend: Examining its suitability as a model*. Palgrave Macmillan.
Willis, P. (1977). *Learning to labor: How working class kids get working class jobs*. Columbia University Press.
Wright, E. O. (2006). Basic income as a socialist project. *Basic Income Studies*.

Wright, E. O. (2010a). *Envisioning real utopias*. Verso.
Wright, E. O. (2010b). *Envisioning real utopias*. Verso.
Wright, E. O. (2019). *How to be an anticapitalist in the twenty-first century*. Verso.
Yates, L. (2015). Rethinking prefiguration: Alternatives, micropolitics and goals in social movements. *Social Movement Studies, 14*(1), 1–21.
Yildiz, O., Rommel, J., Debor, S., Holstenkamp, L., Mey, F., Muller, J. R., Radtke, J., & Rognli, J. (2015). *Financing renewable energy infrastructures via financial citizen participation: The case of Germany*. Springer.
Young, I. M. (2000). *Inclusion and democracy*. Oxford University Press.
Zuboff, S. (2019). *The age of surveillance capitalism*. PublicAffairs.
Zamora, D., (Ed.). (2017). *Against the universal basic income*. Verso.

Index

A
Adorno, Theodor W., 9
Alienation, 4, 7, 9, 12, 39, 63–65, 76–78, 81, 86, 93, 97–98, 101, 106, 108, 113–114, 117–118, 121, 125
  and everyday life, 4, 9, 64, 76, 97, 108
  and labor, 67, 86–87, 93, 101
  and the spectacle, 3, 63–65, 76–78, 86, 93, 97, 108, 114, 125
Anarchism, 13, 113
Atkinson, Anthony B., 43, 81
Autonomist Marxism, 14–15
Autonomy, 1–2, 4–5, 7, 12, 19, 25, 28, 50, 54, 57, 63–64, 67–69, 71, 73, 76, 78, 81, 86, 94, 97, 106, 108, 111, 113–114, 117–118, 123, 125
  Adorno, 9
  advanced capitalism, 1, 25, 106
  and care work, 71
  and council communism, 13
  and decommodification, 19, 64, 67, 76–77, 86, 94, 108, 114
  and ecological sustainability, 29, 55, 69, 124
  and gender/care work, 28, 68, 71
  and institutional reform, 1–2, 4, 63, 117, 124–125
  and May 1968, 14
  and reform coalitions, 42, 58, 115
  and spatial reappropriation, 64, 73, 76, 78, 108, 111, 114
  and temporal liberation, 4, 86, 97, 124
  and urban space, 2, 49
  and working time, 56, 68, 97, 106, 111
  anti-reformism, 6, 107
  as analytical category, 76, 108, 114
  as analytical practice, 4, 76, 108
  as property regime, 5, 50, 54, 68, 73

M. Brum, *Democratic Alternatives*,
https://doi.org/10.1007/978-3-032-23153-6

B
Bauhaus, 7, 11
Benjamin, Walter, 12, 108, 114
Berardi, Franco, 15
Berardi, Franco (Bifo), 15
Boltanski, Luc, 4, 64, 93, 100, 106
Brecht, Bertolt, 12
Buch-hansen, hubert
  background and design, 83
Buch-Hansen, Hubert, 2, 25
  Bauhaus, 7, 11
  cultural, 68, 76, 86

C
Capitalism, 5, 7–8, 10, 14–16, 20, 24–27, 29, 35, 37, 39, 42, 56–57, 59–61, 64, 67, 70, 97, 100, 103–106, 114–115, 119, 121–122
Care work, 41, 43–46, 71, 123
Chiapello, Ève, 4, 64, 93, 100, 106
Climate change and ecology, 25–26, 51, 58
COBRA (art movement), 7
Collective bargaining, 47, 85, 88, 98, 100, 103, 107, 109
Commodification, 8, 10, 14, 16, 38–39, 41–42, 51, 57, 64–65, 68, 73, 76, 78, 86, 101, 113
Commons, 2, 25, 30–31, 37, 52, 56, 59, 61, 69, 71, 101
Cooperatives, 2, 25, 30–31, 33, 35–37, 53–54, 60, 89–92, 95–97, 99–100, 103, 111, 115, 120
  challenges and contradictions, 92
Co-optation and recuperation, 2–4, 6, 13, 15–16, 39, 41, 55, 57, 81, 100, 106
Council communism, 13
COVID-19 pandemic, 24–25, 37, 51, 55, 58, 62, 119
Culture industry, 9
Culture jamming, 12, 16, 60
  calculation debate, 27
  COBRA, 7
  collective bargaining outcomes, 88, 98, 100, 103, 109
  commodity fetishism, 8, 98
  community-controlled, 66, 73
  community-controlled spaces, 66, 73
  contemporary models, 16
  contemporary relevance and renewal, 24
  council communism, 13
  critique of political economy, 8
  digital commons, 25, 30, 56, 59

D
Debord, Guy, 1, 3, 8–9, 11–12, 40, 45, 52, 63–65, 72, 74, 76, 86, 88, 98, 105, 113–114
Decommodification, 6, 18, 68–69, 86, 94, 101
Democratic ownership, 4, 28, 31–34, 36–37, 53–54, 89, 120
Dérive, 2, 11, 45, 48, 71
Détournement, 12, 16, 50, 64, 74, 76–77, 87, 95–96, 107
Digital rights, 61
  dissolution and legacy, 15
  economic, 19, 25, 27, 38, 97, 124
Direct action, 1–2, 60

E
Economic democracy, 28, 32, 38–39, 51, 54, 57, 59, 61, 73, 120–121
Emancipation, 108
Environmental justice, 61, 126
Everyday life, revolution of, 6, 9, 15, 45, 97

Experience economy, 9
ecological dimensions, 27–28, 30

F
Feminism and gender, 10, 20–21, 44, 46, 64, 71, 83, 85, 98, 107–108, 111, 124
Frankfurt School, 9
Functionalist urbanism, 71
founding (1957), 1, 7

G
Global justice movement, 59
Gorz, André, 2–4, 41, 82, 87, 94, 101, 104, 107
Golden Age model, 17
Hardt, Michael, 15
Horkheimer, 9

H
Hardt, Michael, 15
Harvey, David, 9, 12, 15, 22, 48, 72, 82, 87, 103
Horkheimer, max
historical development, 89
Horkheimer, Max, 9
institutional, 74–75
institutional innovations, 26, 90

I
Iceland working time experiment (2015–2019), 83
Immaterial labor, 9
Institutional design, 3–4, 31, 69, 123
Institutional détournement, 74–75, 95, 108, 114
Iceland experiment, 83, 98, 102
institutional design, 31–32, 69, 123
integrated spectacle, 15
internal contradictions, 20
International Movement for an Imaginist Bauhaus, 7
Jackson Rising movement, 61
just transition, 61, 109

J
Jackson Rising movement (Mississippi), 61
key findings, 61

K
Keynesianism, 17–18, 21–22
Keynesian foundations, 17
La Société du Spectacle (1967), 8
Le Corbusier, 11
limitations and context, 88

L
Labor movement, 99, 103, 108
Lazzarato, Maurizio, 9
Le Corbusier, 11
Lefebvre, Henri, 8–9, 12, 15, 48, 70, 72, 87, 94, 101, 108, 114
Lettrist international
lessons and implications, 96
Lettrist International, 7
liberating possibilities, 57
Marcuse, 63, 66, 71, 106
Mondragón, see Mondragón Cooperative, 89

M
Marcuse, Herbert, 9, 66, 106
Market socialism, 5, 26–29, 31–32, 35, 37–38, 89, 121

Markets (as coordination mechanism), 5, 26, 90, 122
Marx, Karl, 8
May 1968, 6, 15
MAY 1968, 14
Mondragón Cooperative Corporation, 32–33, 89
Movement building, 102, 122
  May 1968, 14
  Negri, Antonio, 15
  non-reformist reforms, 2, 4, 96, 107
  Nove on, 28

N
Negri, Antonio, 15
Neoliberalism, 20–22, 37, 42, 103, 116, 119–120
Non-reformist reforms, 2–4, 96, 107
Nove, Alec, 28
  non-reformist reforms (Gorz), 2, 4, 107
  of culture, 8–9, 16, 66, 68, 106
  of everyday life, 9, 45, 50
  of labor, 39–40, 42, 67, 87
  of urban space, 11, 72
  on desire and play, 9–10, 69
  on dérive, 11, 63
  on everyday life, 10, 64
  on psychogeography, 11
  on space and urbanization, 9, 11, 15, 48
  on the poverty of everyday life, 10, 13, 69
  one-dimensional man, 9
  orthodox SI critique, 105–106
  platform capitalism, 66, 114
  platform cooperativism, 30, 35, 60
  political, 20, 61, 68, 73
Nove, alec
  practical examples, 33

P
Participatory action research, 79
Participatory budgeting, 32, 48–49, 70, 73–74, 109
  Porto Alegre, 48
Participatory urbanism, 4, 39, 47, 57, 73
Platform cooperativism, 31, 61
Polanyi, Karl, 81, 99, 116, 122
Political strategy, 58, 74
  preventing co-optation, 108
Porto Alegre, 48
Prefigurative politics, 57, 59–60, 97, 102–103, 113
Private property, 26–27, 51, 60
Psychogeography, 11
  participatory urbanism, 56, 73
  political positions, 13
  practices, 11
  responses to, 107
  Reykjavík, 83
  right to the city, 12, 48, 72
  risks in reform, 4, 6, 38, 56, 58, 115
  Roemer on, 26, 29, 34

R
Race and racial subordination, 64, 71, 101
Redistribution, 2–3, 18, 21, 24, 39
Reform vs. revolution debate, 1
  reform as bridge, 4, 122
Reykjavík (Iceland), 83
Roemer, John, 26, 29, 34, 40
  real utopias, 81, 90
  risks of further commodification, 57, 65
  schweickart on, 3, 29, 32, 52
  schweickart on Roemer, John, 27
  SI legacy in, 13
  situationist analysis of, 93, 101, 108

situationist critique of, 15, 44, 76
SI's anti-reformism, 6, 107
spatial liberation, 47
surveillance capitalism, 16, 27, 31, 61, 67
Roemer, john
spatial liberation, 71

S
Scholz, Trebor, 31, 35, 61
Schweickart, David, 3, 27, 29–30, 32, 52, 121
Self-management, 116, 121
Situationist International (SI), 3, 6–7, 38, 67, 71, 95, 97, 102, 112
Social democracy, 1–3, 5–6, 13, 16, 38, 117–118
sociological transformations, 23
Social movements, 16, 28, 38, 58–60, 65, 75, 77, 97, 101, 103, 108, 116–117, 124
Society of the Spectacle (Debord, 1967), 1, 8, 14, 76
Spatial reappropriation, 71
Spectacle (concept), 1, 3, 6, 8–9, 15, 38, 45, 52, 57, 61, 64–66, 74, 76, 78, 82, 86, 94, 98, 103, 105, 112–113, 125
Srnicek, Nick, 2, 16, 25, 46, 67, 114
Subjectivity, 3, 9, 11, 15, 61, 82, 124
Surveillance capitalism, 16, 27, 31, 61, 67
situationist analysis, 57, 67, 74
suburban sprawl, 72
temporal, 39, 107
theoretical basis, 11–12
theoretical debates, 25
theoretical foundations, 8
Tronti, Mario, 15

T
Temporal liberation, 39, 43, 47, 88, 99, 101, 107
Trade unions, 25, 83
Tronti, Mario, 15
The Revolution of Everyday Life (1967), 9
urban commons, 51, 59

U
Universal Basic Income (UBI), 2, 4, 39, 56–57, 66, 68, 74
Urban planning and space, 2, 11, 15, 47–49, 51, 71–72, 87
Vaneigem on, 9–10, 12, 14, 63–64, 66

V
Vaneigem, Raoul, 2–3, 9–12, 14, 38, 40, 45, 48, 55, 63–64, 66–67, 69, 86–87, 108, 113–114
welfare state and, 17, 19, 39, 86, 115
workers and students, 14

W
Wage labor, 5, 40–42, 45, 57, 68, 92, 101
Weeks, Kathi, 2, 14, 40–41, 86, 88, 97, 99, 102, 106
Welfare state, 17–21, 23, 25, 39, 86, 115–116
Williams, Alex, 46
Worker ownership and self-management, 32–33, 54, 61, 90, 93, 116, 121

Working time reduction, 44–47, 57, 70, 83–85, 87–89, 98–100, 103, 107–109, 111–112, 124
Wright, Erik Olin, 1, 3, 41, 81, 90, 96–97, 99, 103, 107, 114, 116–117, 121–122

Z
Zuboff, Shoshana, 16, 58, 67, 114

The manufacturer's authorised representative in the EU is Springer
Nature Customer Service Centre GmbH, Europaplatz 3, 69115 Heidelberg,
Germany. If you have any concerns regarding our products, please
contact ProductSafety@springernature.com

Printed and bound by CPI Group (UK) Ltd, Croydon, CR0 4YY
16/09/2026
02217792-0006